# LATINO COMMUNITIES

## EMERGING VOICES
### POLITICAL, SOCIAL, CULTURAL, AND LEGAL ISSUES

*Edited by*
Antoinette Sedillo Lopez
University of New Mexico

A ROUTLEDGE SERIES

# TELLING OUR STORIES
## THE LIVES OF MIDWESTERN LATINAS

Theresa Barron-McKeagney

Routledge
New York & London

Published in 2002 by
Routledge
29 West 35th Street
New York, NY 10001

Printed in Great Britain by
Routledge
11 New Fetter Lane
London EC4P 4EE

Routledge is an imprint of the Taylor & Francis Group
Printed in the United States of America on acid-free paper.

10  9  8  7  6  5  4  3  2  1

Cataloging-in-Publication Data for this book is available from the Library
of Congress.

ISBN 0-415-93115-0

To my husband Don
and *mi hijo* Adam Vasquez

# Contents

# List of Figures

# Acknowledgments

T HERE ARE SEVERAL PEOPLE WHO I WOULD LIKE TO SHOW MY RESPECT TO IN THIS acknowledgment. I wish to thank my mentor and advisor, Robert Brown. Dr. Brown has shown me what it means to be a great professor, advisor and listener. He was always there to offer support and guidance through his humility. I will always be indebted to him. The School of Social Work at the University of Nebraska at Omaha specifically Dr. Sunny Andrews-Director, the Faculty and Staff, the former Dean of the College of Public Affairs and Community Service, David Hinton, whose constant support helped me to stay focused on my research regarding these important voices.

I am deeply honored and grateful to the women who agreed to be interviewed for this research, without their patience and understanding, this project could not have been completed. I wish to thank *mi familia,* my immigrant parents, Paul and Chonita whose fortitude and dream to build a better life for them and their children provided strong role modeling for me to follow. A special word of thanks to my mother who began my day when I was a little girl by drinking café con leche with me and by asking, what my "dreams" were, the night before. Therefore, I began each day contemplating my dreams and what visions they predicted to come. What a blessing to learn this truth of dreams from my mother. My deepest respect and thanks to my nine sisters and brothers, who were all my mothers and fathers because I am the youngest (born to our parents long after they thought it was too late to have more children) whose support and bursting pride helped me to finish my writing. The various names that the reader finds in each chapter are the names of my mother, aunt, and sisters. This conscious effort to name my informants after my sisters and aunt brought me ever closer to my family as I wrote their names over and over again in this text. Memories of each sister, my mother and aunt fed me, and soon the informants' cuentos became my sisters' cuentos, and the two were strongly woven together.

I am grateful to *mi cultura* and *todo mi gente* who have shown me great love and support since I joined the Latino community twenty years ago. I continue to reach new heights because their support is my backbone and they are always there to remind me not to forget where I came from and to rely on the voices of my ancestors to help me listen to the stories of others.

Lastly, my deepest love and respect I give to my husband Don and *mi hijo,* my brown-eyed boy, Adam Vasquez. They are forever one in my heart. This work, I dedicate to them.

# TELLING OUR STORIES

CHAPTER 1

# Introduction

## CONTEXT AND THE PROBLEM

THERE ARE APPROXIMATELY 32 MILLION LATINOS/HISPANICS IN THE UNITED STATES in the year 2001. Latino/Hispanic populations may include Central Americans, Latin Americans, Cubans, Puerto Ricans, Spanish Europeans, Mexican and Chicanos. Currently, Latino/Hispanic populations have tripled over the last decade to become perhaps the largest people of color group in the United States. Mexican-Americans account for nearly 65% of the Hispanic population in the United States. (Population Estimates Program, U.S. Census Bureau, 2000). Arias (1986) calls the rapid growth of the Hispanic population in the United States one of the "most compelling social developments in the last 25 years" (p. 27). Latinos now comprise about 12 percent of the total population of the United States. The Latino community in Nebraska is the largest and most rapidly expanding minority population in the state. Latinos number more than 72,000 (4.4 percent) of Nebraska's total population. This population has increased by 94.9 percent according to the 1998 Census data. (Health Status of Racial and Ethnic Minorities in Nebraska: Preliminary Findings October 2000).

Increasingly, there has been more research devoted to studying the Latino population (Bonilla-Santiago 1991; Gracia & De Greiff 2000; Ramirez 1998; Augenbraum & Stavans 1993; Garcia & Zea, 1997; Stanley 1998; Caetano 1986; Cuellar, Harris & Jasso, 1980; Humm-Delgado & Delgado, 1983; Mendoza & Martinez, 1981). These research studies have included topics related to alcohol and drug addiction, psychological interventions, educational issues, acculturation, and cross-cultural studies. There are still few studies, which exclusively focus on Latina women. Blea (1992) stated that until recently female roles in Hispanic and mainstream society have been severely limited (p. 99). Blea (1997) also describes that academic Chicana

3

feminists have tended to define feminism for both Chicanas and Latinas (p. 39). This interesting point may lead many Chicana feminists to take into account class issues as they enter higher academe.

In an analysis of stereotypes of Mexican American women, Andrade (1982) notes that the omission of Latinas (as subjects and researchers) in research has contributed to the invisibility of Latinas. Much research has been devoted to the study of Latinos in general, but little qualitative research in the Midwest specifically has focused on Latinas on any issue. Therefore, according to Andrade (1982) there is a tendency to address programs of research on Mexican American women based on inadequate premises and little attention is given to the interaction between their sex, ethnicity, race, and social class.

Many acculturated Mexican Americans have become largely European American in their way of living, but many have retained knowledge of their traditional culture and speak Spanish. They maintain identification with their own heritage while participating in European American culture. According to Locke (1992), Mexican American culture represents the most constructive and effective means its members have of coping with their changed natural and social environment. An important element to keep in mind is the geographical location of Latinos. Is it easier to maintain an ethnic/racial identity when Latinos' numbers are impressive? In the case of these women in Nebraska, difficulties were encountered due to low percentages of Latinos in this area.

Blea (1992) explains how Chicanas (Mexican-American women) balance two strong cultures. While doing so, they have broken old barriers to reach nontraditional goals and have, in turn, encountered new barriers and new goals. "If studied carefully, the Chicana experience has the potential to guide Anglo, male dominated society in values and redefinition" (p. 89). Cultural blending or being bicultural manifests itself among Chicanas in some highly specific ways (Blea, 1992). "As Chicanas gain access to information, they gain social power. And as they gain social power, the old cultural structures change. As Chicanas gain information, they are able to change their lives" (p. 93).

An increasing number of cultural anthropologists, comparative linguists, and psychologists have theorized that different languages, social structures, rituals, and taboos shape the self differentially in different cultures (Hoare, 1991). Knowledge and identity is developed from within the person and culture in which it is formed. In an analysis of Native American languages, Whorf (1956) stated differences in world-views exist because languages reflect unique metaphysics that arise from their particular grammars and structures. These languages do not merely voice ideas; *they shape and guide concepts and cognition itself.* Authentic understanding of the reality of another involves laying aside one's own interpretations based on assumed reality. As Schweder (1991) stated, "No one can fully flee the bias of his or her own reality to interpret objectively the reality of another" (p. 49).

The inattentiveness by social scientists and other researchers has contributed to the stereotypes that Hoare (1991), Andrade (1982), and Blea (1992) mention. Unintentionally, this lack of understanding continues to promote the invisibility of Latinas in the literature. The premise Whorf supports symbolizes the relationship between culture and language. Latinas who are bilingual and those who are not may see the world through a different lens.

The relevance of this research regarding Latinas' perspectives is critically important, not only to educators, helping professionals and other interested people, but to the Latinas themselves. Understanding their perspectives regarding acculturation and biculturalism, how their families have prepared (or not prepared) them through socialization practices, and the issue of empowerment and how this concept has forged the way for their success, are important concerns for research purposes.

For so long the voices which Latinas have listened to and understood have been "others' voices." Now there exists a medium through which their voices are heard, affected by the "others" indirectly. Many Latina researchers previously mentioned are alarmed that Latinas have been "invisible." There is an image reflected in an old Chinese proverb about how much of a burden it must be to hold the world on one foot, meaning that if only one perspective is known, then the world is out of balance. This proverb exemplifies what this research provides: Latinas' perspectives in the research literature. This qualitative approach ensures that both feet are planted firmly to address these issues holistically.

## STATEMENT OF PURPOSE

The purpose of this study was to understand and bring to life the voices of Latinas (Mexican American) as they interpreted their success. Success was interpreted through their words. Interviews were conducted with Latina women selected from the Omaha and Lincoln, Nebraska area. The meaning of success was interpreted according to the Latinas views of family, self-concept, and community.

## DEFINITIONS

- Latinas: Women of Mexican descent (Chicanas born in the United States or have migrated to the United States before age 7).
- Acculturation: An adjustment process whereby, as a result of sociocultural interactions, a person acquires the customs of an alternate culture (Locke, 1992).
- Biculturalism: Ability to function in the dominant culture while maintaining ties with one's own culture (family of origin culture) (Locke, 1992).
- Socialization: A process by which individuals become members of any system; this process recognizes that Latinas are not socialized into

purely Latino or American culture, but rather into a society where both cultures influence the development of the individual (Martinez, 1988).
- Empowerment Perspective: A process that increases personal, interpersonal and political power so individuals can be proactive in improving their life situations (Gutierrez, 1990).

## DELIMITATIONS

This study was restricted to interviewing Latina women primarily in Omaha and Lincoln, Nebraska. I selected my respondents according to their cultural background (Mexican-American), age (21 through 39 years), and their interest in this topic.

## LIMITATIONS

Possible limitations of this study include:
(1) The Latinas selected were chosen by purposive sampling therefore generalizability is decreased. As noted previously, the women were Mexican American and from Omaha and Lincoln. Some views from other Latina women in other areas of the country could be quite different, so generalizability is not possible. Some of the Latinas selected were acquaintances of the researcher. The researcher also asked Latina women who were not acquaintances to be interviewed.
(2) The ethnographic method may yield different information than that obtained from other research methodologies.

## SIGNIFICANCE OF STUDY

The results of this study could have significance for educators, helping professionals, and community agencies (especially those agencies that work with Latinas). Numerous research studies have focused on Latinos in a wide array of issues but there are very few, if any, qualitative designed research inquiries addressing specifically this topic. This study will help educators better understand the perspectives of Latina women in education by expanding their awareness of Latinas. Helping professionals may be able to utilize an extended assessment tool to capture Latinas' perspectives regarding "empowerment," and how this issue creates a different view for interacting with community. Finally, for community helpers in Latino communities especially, this research could help them identify more "holistic" ways of assisting Latinas with their issues as they define them.

Spradley (1980) stated one way to "synchronize" the needs of people and goals of ethnography is to "consult" with the informants to determine urgent research topics (p. 18). This goal of ethnography is most critical because the informants are the "experts." Addressing this concept culturally would include an understanding of "humilidad" (humility). Humilidad is translated as having a sense of "others" before "self" and being aware of knowing how to be grateful to others for their wisdom. This author steadfastly believes that humilidad is a necessary component to respectfully engage in this type of qualitative research. The significance then for this type of research is to be guided by Latinas' voices. Their voices will no longer be silenced.

Chapter Two presents the reader with a review of related literature regarding Latinas and the issues that the author suggests are critical to an understanding regarding Latinas. Chapter Three describes the methodological approach selected and viewed most appropriate for this study. Chapter Four introduces "las historias" (the life stories) of the Latina women as told in their own voices. Chapter Five presents an analysis of the thematic patterns that emerged in the historias. Chapter Six presents a summary and a discussion of the conclusions of this study of Latinas' historias.

## REFERENCES

Andrade, S. (1982). Social Science Stereotypes of the Mexican American Woman: Policy Implications for Research. Hispanic Journal of Behavioral Sciences, 4(2), 223–244.

Arias, M.B. (1986). The Context of Education for Hispanic Students: An Overview. American Journal of Education, 95, 26–57.

Augenbraum, H. & Stavans, I. (1993). Growing Up Latino. Boston: Houghton Miflin Company.

Blea, I. (1997). U.S. Chicanas and Latinas Within a Global Context: Women of Color at the Fourth World Women's Conference. Westport, CT: Praeger.

Blea, I. (1992). La Chicana and the Intersection of Race, Class, and Gender. New York: Praeger Press.

Bonilla-Santiago, G. (1991). Hispanic Women Breaking New Ground Through Leadership. Latino Studies Journal, 2, 19–37.

Caetano, R. (1986). Patterns and Problems of Drinking Among U.S. Hispanics. In U.S. Department of Health and Human Services, Report of the Secretary's Task Force on Black and Minority Health. Volume VII, Chemical Dependency and Diabetes (pp. 143–186) (DHHS Publication No. 85–487). Washington, DC: U.S. Government Printing Office.

Cuellar, I., Harris, L.C., & Jasso, R. (1980). An Acculturation Rating Scale for Mexican American Normal and Clinical Populations. Hispanic Journal of Behavioral Sciences, 2, 199–217.

Garcia, J.G. & Zea, M.C. (1997). Psychological Interventions and Research with Latino Populations. Boston: Allyn and Bacon.

Gracia, Jorge, J.E. & Greiff, P. (2000). Hispanics/Latinos in the United States. New York: Routledge.

Gutierrez, Lorraine M. (1990). Working with Women of Color: An Empowerment Perspective. Social Work. March. 149–153.

Hoare, C. (1991). Psychosocial Identity Development and Cultural Others. Journal of Counseling and Development. September/October 1991, 70, 45–53.

Humm-Delgado, D. & Delgado, M. Hispanic Adolescents and Substance Abuse: Issues for the 1980s. In Adolescent Substance Abuse (pp. 71–85). Haworth Press, 1983.

Locke, Don C. (1992). Increasing Multicultural Understanding. Newbury Park, CA: Sage.

Martinez, Marcos, A. (1988). Toward A Model of Socialization for Hispanic Identity: The Case of Mexican-Americans. In Pastora San Juan Cafferty & W.L. McCready (Eds.), Hispanics in the United States. New Jersey: Transaction Books.

Mendoza, R.H., & Martinez, J.L. (1981). The Measurement of Acculturation. In A. Baron Jr. (Ed.), Exploration in Chicano Psychology. New York: Holt Press.

Nebraska Department of Health and Human Services Preventive and Community Health. (2000). Health Status of Racial and Ethnic Minorities in Nebraska: Preliminary Findings.

Ramirez, M. III. (1998). Multicultural/Multiracial Psychology: Mestizo Perspectives in Personality and Mental Health. Northvale, NJ: Jason Aronson Inc.

Schweder, R.A. (1991). Thinking Through Cultures. Cambridge: Harvard University Press.

Spradley, James. P. 1980. Participant Observation. Macalester College: Holt, Rinehart, and Winston, Inc.

Stanley, S.K. (1998). Other Sisterhoods. Chicago: University of Illinois Press.

U.S. Bureau of the Census, U.S. Population Estimates Program, Population Division. (2000, October). Resident Population Estimates of the United States by Sex, Race, and Hispanic Origin: April 1, 1990 to July 1, 1999, with Short-Term Projection to September 1, 2000. Washington, DC: U.S. Government Printing Office.

Whorf, B.L. (1956). Science and Linguistics. In J.B. Carrroll (Ed.), Language, Thought, and Reality (pp. 212–213). Cambridge: Technology Press of Massachusetts Institute of Technology.

# CHAPTER 2

# Literature Review

T HIS CHAPTER EXAMINES THE LITERATURE RELATED TO THREE CONCEPTS: acculturation/biculturalism, socialization, and empowerment perspectives as they specifically relate to Latinas.

## ACCULTURATION/BICULTURALISM

Acculturation and its measurement in Latinos has been studied more intensely among social scientists (Torres-Matrullo, 1980). Acculturation is a multidimensional phenomenon, which has diverse definitions. Acculturation has been defined as the degree of identification and integration with the majority culture (Sunberg, 1981). Acculturation has also been considered dual cultural membership or biculturalism. Ramirez and Castañeda (1974) contend that each culture possesses distinct cognitive styles by which it relates to and organizes the world. These authors propose that Mexican Americans are bicultural. Although there are numerous acculturation studies (Annis, 1974; Berry, 1980; Curtis, 1990; Griffith, 1983; Torres-Matrullo, 1980) there are only two that specifically investigate the relationship between traditionalism and acculturation in Mexican-American women (Satterfield, 1966; Tharp, Meadow, Lennhoff & Satterfield, 1968).

Social scientists propose several definitions of acculturation. Berry and Annis (1974) view acculturation as a product of interacting systems which include ecological-cultural-behavioral frameworks influenced by mainstream (dominant) culture in the United States. The more opportunities an individual shares with this dominant culture, the more likely the influence will be in education, values, and family roles. Berry (1980) believes acculturation is not unidirectional only (e.g., person of color assimilating to mainstream culture). Acculturation should be measured by two processes: (1) the degree of assimilation to the dominant culture and, (2) the degree of retention to their own culture. Ruiz and Padilla (1977) comment that each Latino person, in addition to being a member of the Latino culture and some smaller Latino subgroup (i.e., Mexican-American, Cuban, Puerto Rican), is also a member of the dominant culture. The authors state, ". . . the degree of acculturation can be inferred from degree of commitment to cultural variables; that is, language values, tradition, diet and costume" (p. 175).

Kranau, Green and Valencia-Weber (1982) investigated the relationship of acculturation to the variables of attitudes toward women, sex-role attribution, sex- role behaviors and demographics in Latina women. Their findings indicated a positive correlation between greater acculturation and liberal attitudes toward women, single status, more education, and younger ages. Greater acculturation was negatively correlated with more feminine household behaviors. Kranau et al. (1982) stated if research is focused on Latinas and acculturation, then one must be aware of the "range of acceptable behaviors for individuals in that culture" (p. 22). The authors agree changes for women in the white dominant culture have had direct and indirect impact upon Latinas. Blea (1997) suggests that defining Chicanas should not be within a limited context. Chicanas are products of their environments, their ancestry and the historical-social-political era that they are born into. Blea also contends that the real trailblazers are those who "rebel and struggle for change." These are the women whom Blea (1997) suggests "leave a distinguished legacy" (p. 42).

The various levels of acculturation that Latinas experience has a profound effect on the way in which they see their worlds. A Latina who is assimilated fully into the mainstream dominant culture may not realize what Latino culture contributes to the mainstream. Helms (1990) discusses a model of racial identity. Stage One refers to the individual's unequivocal preference for dominant cultural values over those of his or her own culture. In Stage Three, Latinas could be so absorbed with the Latino culture that other cultures are viewed as insignificant, Helms refers to this stage as resistance and immersion. The final stage is synergetic articulation and awareness where individuals experience positive self- regard for their cultural identity and appreciation for other cultures.

Griffith (1983) contended that biculturalism is the most psychosocially healthy orientation for immigrant Mexicans to the United States. Helms' final stage appears to support a bicultural perspective. Ramirez (1984) stated that bicultural people ". . . have extensive socialization and life experiences in two or more cultures and participate actively in these cultures" (p. 82). The bicultural person is flexible, can problem solve using methods from differing cultural perspectives, and is adaptable in behavior. These attitudes and behaviors are highly desirable in the United States.

## SOCIALIZATION

The Mexican family is viewed by social scientists as being patriarchal (Diaz-Guerrero, 1955; Martinez, 1988). The woman in the family devotes herself entirely to "la familia" (the family) while denying her own needs in the process. Academic and professional success by females accomplished outside the home is discouraged. These controversial definitions of the Mexican family have caused many social scientists to reevaluate the research regarding the family. Cotera (1976) stated that inappropriate research tools, methodologies, and examiner bias have perpetuated stereotypes and destructive inaccurate accounts regarding Latino families. Social scientists see Latino families as an insulated group that continues traditions and customs despite residence of several generations in the United States (Kiev, 1972; Sabogal, 1987). American influence is changing the Latino family through education, military service, housing patterns, employment, and politics (Padilla & Ruiz, 1973).

With the exception of Comas-Diaz and Greene (1994) whose work on women of color contributes to the importance of integrating ethnic and gender identities in psychotherapy, the research literature regarding Latinas and psychological approaches is limited. Senour (1977) expressed that psychological literature relating directly to the Latina is extremely confined. She is dismayed that this obvious omission, ". . . undoubtedly reflects a lack of interest on the part of social scientists" (p. 329). Senour (1977) believes that the Chicana is a product of two cultures: American and Mexican. A summary of her findings indicate psychological differences between Mexican-American males and females which lead to greater oppression for females. Chicanas' personality characteristics reveal lower self esteem, more field dependence sensitivity (the organization of a field as a whole, dominates perception of its parts), greater identification with families, more concern with their physical selves, fewer well defined psychic selves, more death dreams, and depression (p. 337). Becerra (1982) and Canino (1982) stated there is evidence of Latina women in the United States being a high-risk group for developing mental illness. They describe depressed socioeconomic conditions, as well as role conflicts as a result of migration and acculturation which contribute to jeopardizing Latinas' well being. This information regarding Chicanas should be quite alarming to helping professionals.

Zuniga (1988) advises helping professionals to develop "culturally syntonic" skills to assist Chicanas. The definition of culturally syntonic skills refers to services that address specific cultural perspectives, preferences, and needs of Latinas. Zuniga addresses the issues related to family responsibility, role conflict, and identity confusion. She suggests "familial assessments" to help understand how Latinas cope with some of these issues. She identifies a core socializing theme in some families is the expectation that Mexican American children will contribute to the welfare of the family, thus promoting a collective sense of family responsibility enabling members to turn to one another for support and resources.

Much of the literature by women of color about women of color attempts to counteract the stereotypes and negative images, which endure and imbed themselves in the research (Andrade, 1982; Blea, 1992; Ybarra, 1983). Many Latinas live with feelings of powerlessness, alienation, and images of themselves which are sexist and racist in nature (Blea, 1992). It is testament to the strengths of Latinas that they are able to survive in these environments and function at highly motivated levels; they are achievers, personable, capable and powerful. These qualities may be a product of their biculturalism that empowers them to overcome significant barriers.

## THEORETICAL ORIENTATIONS

Many theoretical models are based on Western models of socialization that ignore important variables that influence the socialization process which comprise history, cultural differences, and socioeconomic status (Martinez, 1981). Martinez offers a model of socialization practices, which emphasizes the integration of development and systems theories. Garza and Lipton (1982) propose there is an urgent need for a theoretical model that can incorporate the interactional effects of culture and personality within a multicultural context. Kluckhohn (1961) compared five cultures with respect to cultural values and world-views. The five cultures were: Mormons, Homesteaders, Spanish-Americans, Zuni, and Navajo. There were several questions asked regarding cultural values. Some of the questions and answers by the Spanish-American group included:

> "Are the needs of self more important than the needs of others?"
> Response: Other
> "How much is dependence viewed to carry over into adulthood or how much is adulthood viewed as autonomous?" Response: Dependence
> "Is the individual actively assertive or quietly accepting?" Response: Acceptant
> "Is conformity to the discipline of rules sought or is fulfillment sought by breaking away from rules?" Response: Fulfillment by breaking away from rules

Locke (1992) states that Mexican Americans assign higher value to life activities that may be in contrast to European Americans.

> It is through physical and mental well-being and through an ability to experience, in response to environment, emotional feelings and to express these to one another and share these, that one experiences the greatest rewards and satisfactions in life. It is much more valuable to experience things directly, through intellectual awareness and

emotional involvement, than indirectly, through remembering past accomplishments or accumulating wealth. The philosopher, poet, musician, and artist are more often revered in this culture than the business person or financier (p. 140).

Martinez (1986) specifically addresses family socialization patterns of Mexican Americans. Similar to Berry's ecological-cultural-behavioral dynamics in acculturation, Martinez' refers to Vggotsky's sociohistorical approach that features the individual, microsocial and macrosocial levels of analysis. Martinez addresses four "urgent needs" that social scientists must consider in their research on Latino families with special focus on socialization patterns: "(1) research needs integration, (2) research must be multivariate and foster interdisciplinary perspectives, (3) the need to develop sound theoretical constructs, and (4) the need to provide positive characterizations of Mexican American children, families and communities" (p. 264).

Rueschenberg and Buriel (1989) investigated the relationship of acculturation to family functioning and socialization. They viewed this dynamic from a systems perspective that included an analysis of internal and external factors. They concluded that Mexican American families adapt to these interactions using coping techniques which are "external" when interacting with others outside the family, and "internal" mechanisms when interacting within the family. They believed patterns of functioning or socialization continue to endure despite influence by mainstream society. Their results appear to confirm that for many Latino families, acculturation and socialization patterns may be strengthened by a bicultural viewpoint.

## EMPOWERMENT PERSPECTIVES/SUCCESS

Empowerment is a process of increasing personal, interpersonal, or political power so individuals can act to improve their life situations (Gutierrez, 1990). Empowerment theory is based on a conflict model that assumes there are groups in society which maintain and control access to various institutions. Individual empowerment contributes to group empowerment. This increase in the group's power enhances the functioning of individual members (Rappaport, 1985). To understand empowerment and Latinas, a group development perspective is helpful.

Ramirez (1990) addresses two complementary concepts: adult education principles and their application to community development. Ramirez views the role of educators and counselors as facilitators for community development and community empowerment. Both concepts share similar objectives which create and enhance self direction, self-reliance, and sustain learning and self empowerment. Ramirez believes certain conditions must be recognized for adult education concepts to be applied to community development/empowerment/role of educators and counselors: (1) the power relationships and institutional structures; (2) community dynamics, and (3) the role of the educator/counselor. These three conditions exemplify the interactive relationship between community empowerment (developed from personal empowerment) and understanding personal roles.

Unfortunately, not enough research has been generated specifically addressing empowerment perspectives regarding Latinas. Academic success is viewed by many as a form of empowerment. Gandara (1982) attempted to isolate the factors of "success" in higher education for high achieving Latinas. Her study consisted of interviewing professional women who had their Ph.D's, MD's, and JD's. Latinas reported the support for their achievement included role modeling by their mothers, discipline strategies that reflected taking responsibility for behavior, and their attendance at integrated schools where they competed with mainstream students. Academically successful Chicanas find it important to receive support by identifying with their cultural background (Vasquez, 1982). Buriel (1982) explained that acculturating Mexican Americans who maintain a tie with their traditional culture are better able to "inoculate" themselves against general negative images of Mexican Americans. Blea examines similar inequities in the research addressing little attention that has been given to her power, her cultural achievements, her successes and her social rewards, she adds, "She is a woman whose life is too often characterized by poverty, racism and sexism not only in the dominant culture, but also within her own culture" (1997, p. 15). These studies reveal that empowerment perspectives and strategies enhance Latinas' attitude toward success and support the integration between success and family obligation. In a similar perspective, Bonilla-Santiago (1991) addressed the neglect that Latinas have witnessed in response to their leadership abilities. Bonilla-Santiago prepared a monograph on the relationship between Latinas and their backgrounds, including education, employment, career goals and cultural differences as they prepared for leadership opportunities. Leadership opportunities have been scarce for Latinas, so Latinas have adapted by developing their own culturally relevant cohort system which includes, informal mentoring and dialogue with Latinas, accessing power relationships through community work and attaining higher educational levels.

## SUMMARY

There has been research generated regarding Latinos in many life issues. Generally there has been little research, especially qualitative, which introduces concepts and approaches regarding Latina women and their perceptions of success. Their perspectives on family, community, self-concept, and success have historically been measured in outcomes and products. Research generated in this fashion tends to minimize and detach the rich, thick description so frequently found in qualitative research. This research is unique because it provides the readers (educators, helping professionals, and interested others) with an intimate perspective of Latinas' lives through their own words, and their own images of success.

Words are very powerful mediums through which we communicate our most private thoughts. The research in this study, through a qualitative approach, brought those words to life in a much richer and multifaceted way. Understanding qualitative research through an intuitive lens is necessary for this study. Utilizing a holistic approach which commits to Latinas' voices as "expert" is a fundamental principle of qualitative research (Bogden & Biklen, 1992). Integrating three concepts, acculturation/biculturalism, socialization, and empowerment to understand Latinas realities is a fresh approach which is worthy of qualitative research.

## REFERENCES

Andrade, S. (1982). Social Science Stereotypes of the Mexican American Woman: Policy Implications for Research. Hispanic Journal of Behavioral Sciences, 4(2), 223–244.

Becerra, R.M., Karno, M., & Escobar, J.I. (1982). The Hispanic Patient: Mental Health Perspectives. New York: Grune and Stratton, Inc.

Berry, J.W. (1980). Acculturation as Varieties of Adaptation. In A.M. Padilla (Ed.), Acculturation: Theory, Models, and Some New Findings. Boulder, CO: Westview Press.

Berry, J.W., & Annis, R.C. (1974). Acculturative Stress: The Role of Ecology, Culture, and Differentiation. Journal of Cross-Cultural Psychology, 5, 382–406.

Blea, I. (1997). U.S. Chicanas and Latinas Within a Global Context: Women of Color at the Fourth World Women's Conference. Westport, CT: Praeger.

Blea, I. (1992). La Chicana and the Intersection of Race, Class, and Gender. New York: Praeger Press.

Bogden, R.C., & Bilken, S.K. (1992). Qualitative Research for Education. Needham Heights, MA: Allyn and Bacon.

Buriel, R. (1982). Relationship of Traditional Mexican American Culture to Adjustment and Delinquency Among Three Generations of Mexican American Male Adolescents. Hispanic Journal of Behavioral Sciences, 1, 41–55.

Bonilla-Santiago, Gloria. (1991). Hispanic Women Breaking New Ground Through Leadership. Latino Studies Journal, 2, 19–37.

Canino, G. (1982). The Hispanic Woman: Sociocultural Influences on diagnoses and treatment. In R.M. Becerra, M. Karno & J.I. Escobar (Eds.), Mental Health and Hispanic Americans (pp. 117–137). New York: Grune and Stratton, Inc.

Comas-Diaz., L., & Greene, B. (1994). Women of Color with Professional Status. In L. Comas-Diaz & B. Greene (Eds.), Women of Color: Integrating ethnic and gender identities in psychotherapy (pp. 347–388). New York: Guilford Press.

Cotera, M. Profile on the Mexican American Woman. Austin, Texas: National Educational Laboratory, 1976.

Curtis, P.A. (1990). The Consequences of Acculturation to Service Delivery and Research with Hispanic Families. Child and Adolescent Social Work Journal, 7(2), 147–159.

Diaz-Guerrero, R. (1955). Neurosis and the Mexican Family Structure. American Journal of Psychiatry, 112, 411–417.

Gandara, P. (1982). Passing through the eye of the needle: High Achieving Chicanas. Hispanic Journal of Behavioral Sciences, 4(2), 167–179.

Garza, R.T., & Lipton, J.P. (1982). Theoretical Perspectives on Chicano Personality Development. Hispanic Journal of Behavioral Sciences, 4(4), 407– 432.

Griffith, J. (1983). Relationship Between Acculturation and Psychological Impairment in Adult Mexican Americans. Hispanic Journal of Behavioral Sciences, 5, 431–459.

Helms, J.E. (1990). Black and White Racial Identity: Theory, Research, and Practice. New York: Greenwood Press.

Kiev, A. (1972). Transcultural Psychiatry. New York: The Free Press.

Kluckhohn, F.R. & Strodtbeck, F.L. (1961). Variations in Value Orientations. Evanston, IL: Row, Patterson, & Co.

Kranua, E.J., Green, V. & Valencia-Weber, G. (1982). Acculturation and the Hispanic Woman: Attitudes Toward Women, Sex-Role Attribution, Sex-Role Behavior, and Demographics. Hispanic Journal of Behavioral Sciences, 4(1), 21– 40.

Locke, Don C. (1992). Increasing Multicultural Understanding. Newbury Park, CA: Sage.

Martinez, M.A. (1981). Conversational Asymmetry Between Mexican Mothers and Children. Hispanic Journal of Behavioral Sciences, 3, 329–346.

Martinez, M.A. (1986). Family Socialization Among Mexican-Americans. Human Development, 29, 264–279.

Martinez, Marcos A. (1988). Toward A Model of Socialization for Hispanic Identity: The Case of Mexican- Americans. In Pastora San Juan Cafferty & W.L. McCready (Eds.), Hispanics in the United States. New Jersey: Transaction Books.

Padilla, A.M. & Ruiz, R.A. Latino Mental Health: A Review of the Literature. National Institute of Mental Health, Washington, DC: U.S. Government Printing Office, 1973.

Ramirez, M., & Castaneda, A. (1974). Cultural Democracy, Bicognitive Development, and Education. New York: Academic Press.

Ramirez, M. (1984). Assessing and Understanding Biculturalism- Multiculturalism in Mexican-American Adults. In J.L. Martinez & R.H. Mendoza (Eds.), Chicano Pyschology, 2nd Ed. (pp. 77–94) Orlando, FL: Academic Press.

Ramirez, R. (1990). The Application of Adult Education to Community Development. Community Development Journal, 23(2), 131–138.

Rappaport, J. (1985). The Power of Empowerment Language. Social Policy, 17(2), 15–21.

Rueschenberg, E., & Buriel, R. (1989). Mexican American Family Functioning and Acculturation: A Family Systems Perspective. Hispanic Journal of Behavioral Sciences, 11(3), 232–244.

Sabogal, F.G., Marin, R. Otero-Sabogal, B.V. Marin, & E.J. Perez-Stable. (1987). Hispanic Familism and Acculturation: What changes and what doesn't? Hispanic Journal of Behavioral Sciences, 9, 397–412.

Satterfield, D.M. Acculturation and marriage role patterns: A comparative study of Mexican American Women. Unpublished doctoral dissertation, University of Arizona, 1966.

Senour, M.N. (1977). Psychology of the Chicana. In J.L. Martinez (Ed.), Chicano Psychology. New York: Academic Press.

Sundberg, N.D. (1981). Cross-Cultural Counseling and Psychotherapy: A Research Overview. In A.J. Marsella and P.B. Pederson (Eds.), Cross-Cultural Counseling and Psychotherapy. New York: Pergamon Press.

Tharp, R.G., Meadow, A., Lennhoff, S.G., & Satterfield, D.M. (1968). Changes in marriage roles accompanying the acculturation of the Mexican American wife. Journal of Marriage and the Family, 30, 404–412.

Torres-Matrullo, C.M. (1980). Acculturation, sex-role values and mental health among mainland Puerto Ricans. In A.M. Padilla (Ed.), Acculturation: Theory, Models, and Some New Findings. Boulder, CO: Westview Press.

Vasquez, M. (1982). Confronting Barriers to the Participation of Mexican- American Women in Higher Education. Hispanic Journal of Behavioral Sciences, 4(2), 147–165.

Ybarra, L. (1983). Empirical and Theoretical Developments in the Study of Chicano Families. In A. Valdez, A. Camarillo, and T. Almaguer (Eds.), The State of Chicano Research on Family, Labor, and Migration. Stanford: Stanford Center for Chicano Research.

CHAPTER 3

# Approach

T HIS CHAPTER PRESENTS THE METHODOLOGY FOR THIS STUDY. THE AUTHOR FOL-
lowed a life history approach and utilized ethnography processes for
gathering information.

## THE ETHNOGRAPHIC RESEARCH DESIGN

This attempt to study Latina women utilizes the ethnographic research tradition. This design emerged from the field of anthropology. "Ethnographic
fieldwork is the hallmark of cultural anthropology" (Spradley, 1980, p. 3).
Ethnography is the work of describing a culture. Culture to many signifies
identification with a group, values, norms, traditions, customs, and symbol-
ic relationships (Locke, 1991).

> By identifying cultural knowledge as fundamental, we have merely
> shifted the emphasis from behavior and artifacts to their meaning.
> The ethnographer observes behavior but goes beyond it to inquire
> about the meaning of that behavior. The ethnographer sees artifacts
> and natural objects but goes beyond them to discover what meanings
> people assign to these objects. The ethnographer observes and records
> emotional states but goes beyond them to discover the meaning of
> feelings (Spradley, 1980, p. 7).

Jacob (1987) discusses "holistic ethnography" which describes cultures
from an integrative perspective. She states ". . . holistic ethnographers frequently have an attitude of exploration and learning rather than one of test-
ing" (p. 12). Holistic ethnography is appropriate for this study because the
goal is to understand a unique circumstance (perception of success) through
analysis of patterns and themes that Latinas express. Watson and Watson-

19

Franke (1985) state that the life history approach utilizes methods grounded in hermeneutic phenomenology which take into account subjective experience of the informant as a phenomenon in its own right. "In other words, phenomenology is the systematic attempt to uncover and describe the structures, the internal meaning structures, of lived experience" (Watson, et al., 1985, p. 10). Van Manen (1990) encourages scholars of the hermeneutic phenomenological perspective to understand the difference between intellectually comprehending this approach and actually "actively do it" (p. 8). The phenomenological approach is concerned with meaning and subjective truth. In life history studies, the implication is that the author convey not only the story of the informant's life, but her or his own epistemological assumptions which contributed to the life story.

## THE RESEARCHER'S ROLE

The role of the researcher in qualitative research is the primary data collection instrument. The researcher also needs to identify personal values, assumptions, and biases at the outset of the study. The researcher needs to be prepared for the unexpected, even when research questions are clear, something spontaneous could occur (Marshall & Rossman, 1989). My knowledge of Latinas and their perceptions of success come from my intimate knowledge of Latinas because I am a Latina. I feel that I understand what being a Latina symbolizes. Although I realize that I cannot possibly understand all the multifaceted dimensions there are that accompanies being Latina in this country. My work in this area is so liberating. I am in constant vigilance regarding the stories of these Latinas, thus it is sometimes difficult to provide the reader with assumptions and analyses about their lived experiences.

Through my work, I have some feeling that I know what academic success implies. My question though is not only about "academic success" but how success is seen through the eyes of "self," "family," and "community." It would be improper and limiting if I only interpreted "success" through academic achievement.

I bring a personalized and attentive structure to this process where Latinas' voices are heard in a context that is evolving. When I wrote my dissertation eight years ago, qualitative research regarding Latinas seemed nonexistent. Because of my intimate contacts with many Latinas, this ethnographic approach was unique. The understanding and the art of listening that I believe I possess, gently nurtured Latinas to speak of their personal perspectives on their lives. The relationship between the women and me is comparable to being a "close intimate," in Spanish, the word is "comadre," and the style is "confianza" (trust). In our shared reality as Latinas, no detailed explanation is necessary for understanding these Latinas' perspectives. This is exciting for me and I hope that it will be for others. To see into the hearts and minds of some adult Latinas through an intuitive process will be enlightening for educators, helping professionals, and others. Lama Surya Das

(1997) wrote that "intrinsic awareness is the common denominator of all sentient beings (p. 48)." Through these cuentos, the reader can grasp an understanding of the sense of "community" which affects the women. Their awareness of being uniquely Latina assists their transcendence and illumination. Lama Surya Das suggests that this illumination along with the power of compassionate action can heal the world.

Particular attention was given to the perceptions of success that Latina informants discussed and how these perceptions related to everyday living through understanding self, family, community, and work. I am a Latina, therefore, I may bring certain biases to my research. Although I attempted to ensure objectivity, these biases may have shaped my perceptions and the way I interpreted my experiences with the Latinas. Research of this nature is so unique (I believe that this research is the first of its kind in the Midwest and possibly much of the United States) perhaps my biases should not be considered as inappropriate. I did whatever was in my power not to cross critical boundaries which would cause discomfort for these Latinas. I believe I possess strong intuitive and helping professional strengths which I owe to my upbringing in my family of origin as well as my training as a social worker. These skills enabled me to interview these women in a most responsible and respectful fashion.

## BOUNDING THE STUDY AND DATA COLLECTION

### Events

Using ethnographic research and life history methodology, the focus of this study was on the everyday experiences, meaningful events of Latinas, and the perceptions and meaning attached to those experiences as expressed by the women. Special attention was given to those perceptions that shaped the Latinas' positions regarding success through self-awareness, family and community. A quality of ethnography is to approach situations from a holistic perspective that implies concern for interacting systems. In this study, the author concentrated on how Latinas interpreted success with a holistic understanding of self, family, work and community.

### Setting

This study was conducted in places selected by the informants. These interviews were conducted in their homes. The informants were selected via purposeful sampling. Purposive sampling selects informants based upon what they can bring to the research and facilitate the expansion of the developing theory (Bogden & Biklen, 1992, p. 71). The geographical area is in the Midwest, specifically the Omaha and Lincoln, Nebraska areas. Some of the women selected were acquaintances of the researcher and others were recommended to the researcher.

## Informants

The informants in this study were nine Latinas (women who are Mexican American). I realize that this subgroup's population numbers are significantly higher in this region than other subgroups which include Mexicans, Puerto Ricans, Cubans, Central and South Americans. The women were first (native born Mexican but came to the United States before age seven), second (parents born in Mexico, but informants born in the United States), and third generation (both parents and Latinas born in the United States). They have lived most of their lives in the Midwest. The age range spans 17 years. The women's ages were from 21 to 38.

## The Grand Tour Question

How do Latinas perceive themselves through self-reflection, family, community, and work (work can be inside or outside the home) when they contemplate success?

## Sub Questions

- Is self-concept a reflection of Latinas' family socialization patterns?
- Is this perception of self reflected through acculturation/biculturation patterns?
- Does this perception of self reflect an affiliation with the community, in this case, the Latino community?
- To what do these women attribute their success to: self-empowerment, family, community?
- What is the holistic picture which emerges from the perception of these three systems coming together, if they do?

### DATA COLLECTION AND ANALYSIS

Data were collected from February through June 1993. This included one and two hour interviews with the selected informants. Nine women were selected out of twelve interviewed. These nine women were chosen based on the strength of their interviews; three were excluded because they did not meet the criteria previously discussed. One woman came to the United States later than age 7 and returned not much later to attend school in Mexico and then returned to the United States around age 17–18. The researcher felt that this informant's socialization consisted of a more Mexican national upbringing than the Mexican-American experience. The two other informants' interviews were equally as strong as those selected but not as long. The author therefore selected those interviews with the most information. Protocol for interviews were open and unstructured questions. To assist in the data collection phase I tape-recorded the informants' life histories. I utilized a field log, providing a detailed account of the interview and the site. I recorded details related to my observations in a personal journal to understand my feelings throughout this research study.

## Procedures

Merriam (1988) and Marshall and Rossman (1989) contend that data collection and data analysis must be a simultaneous process in qualitative research. Schatzman and Strauss (1973) claim that qualitative data analysis primarily entails classifying things, persons, and events and the properties that characterize them. Typically throughout the data analysis process, ethnographers index or code their data using as many categories as possible (Jacob, 1987). They seek to identify and describe patterns and themes from the perspective of the participant(s), then attempt to understand and explain these patterns and themes (Agar, 1980). During data analysis the data were organized categorically and chronologically, reviewed repeatedly, and continually coded. A list of major ideas that surfaced were chronicled (Merriam, 1988). Taped interviews were transcribed verbatim. Field notes were regularly reviewed.

In addition, the data analysis process was aided with a qualitative data analysis computer program called Textbase Alpha (Tesch, 1989). This software program was designed to assist the researcher in organizing qualitative data for analysis. Through its operation, Textbase Alpha helps to organize and clarify tasks in qualitative research that in the past has been cumbersome for researchers. The previous task of cutting and pasting important passages has been replaced by the Textbase Alpha program. This program eliminates those tedious tasks and the researcher is free to develop the intellectual centerpiece of their research. The Textbase Alpha program attends to two basic functions: attaching codes to segments of text and searching through the data for segments coded in certain manners and combining them (see Appendix). This software program was utilized by the author to code informants' life histories, and organize and sort special thematic patterns.

## Verification

The researcher attempted to insure internal validity. The following strategies were employed:

1. Professional mentor checking - the researcher sought professional opinions by professional mentors who are involved with research regarding Latinas and Latinos (Dr. Rusty Barcelo- University of Iowa, Dr. James Ramirez- The Omaha Public Schools and Dr. Miguel Carranza- University of Nebraska- Lincoln),
2. Member checking - some of the informants were asked to review their transcribed interview and give feedback on the written text of their life history, to assist the researcher in understanding that the meaning of this text was truthful of their reality,

3. Clarification of researcher bias - at the outset of this study researcher bias was articulated in writing under the heading, "The Researcher's Role."

The primary strategy utilized in this research to ensure external validity was the provision of rich, thick, detailed descriptions so anyone interested in transferability will have a comparable framework for association (Merriam, 1988). Three techniques were employed in this study. First, the researcher provided a detailed account of the focus of the study, the researcher's role, the informants' position and base for selection, and the context from which data was gathered (Goetz & LeCompte, 1984). Second, professional mentors who are Latinos were asked to give their insights on this text, and provide the researcher with personal opinions of this type of research on both professional academic levels and as members of Mexican-American culture. Finally, data collection and analysis strategies are reported in detail to provide a clear and accurate picture of the methods used in this study. All phases of this project were subject to scrutiny by external auditors who are experienced in qualitative research methods (namely, Dr. John Creswell at the University of Nebraska-Lincoln).

## Ethical Considerations

Most authors who discuss qualitative research design address the importance of ethical considerations (Bogden & Biklen, 1992; Marshall & Rossman, 1989; Spradley, 1980). The researcher has an obligation to respect the rights, needs, values, and desires of the informant(s). To an extent, ethnographic research is always obtrusive. Participant observation invades the life of the informant (Spradley, 1980) and sensitive information is frequently revealed. Dr. Felix Padilla, a sociologist, formerly at the University of Chicago, embarked on a journey of ethnographic research that led him into the "world of gangs" in Southside Chicago. He recalled at first what it felt like being an "outsider" though the gang membership was mostly Puerto Rican and he was too, he felt this bond was not strong enough, he was not part of the gang structure. He explained his research to several Latino doctoral students who attended a seminar at UCLA about what ethnography symbolized. Toward the end of his research, he really felt like "one of them" (UCLA, June 1990). Ethnographic research has traditionally been undertaken in fields that, by virtue of the contrast between them and the researcher's own culture, could be described as "exotic" (Marshall & Rossman, 1989). This is particularly important when interviewing Latina women who historically have not been called upon for their expert viewpoints. Thus, there may be some reluctance, and rightly so, by Latina women to engage in a discussion about their lives.

The following safeguards were implemented to protect the informants' rights: 1) the research objectives were articulated verbally and in writing so that they were clearly understood by the informant (including a description of how data will be used), 2) written permission to proceed with the study as articulated was received from the informant, 3) a research exemption form was filed with the University of Nebraska Institutional Review Board, 4) the informants were informed of all data collection devices and activities, 5) verbatim transcriptions and written interpretations and reports were available to the informants, 6) the informants' rights, interests and wishes were considered first when choices were made regarding data, and 7) the final decision regarding informant anonymity rested with the informant.

## Reporting the Findings

Miles and Huberman (1984) address the importance of creating a data display and suggest that narrative text has been the most frequent form of display for qualitative data. This is a naturalistic study, therefore, the results are presented in descriptive, narrative form rather than as a quantitative report. Thick description (Bogden & Bilken, 1992) is the vehicle for communicating a holistic picture of the experiences of Latina women. When culture is examined from this perspective, the ethnographer is faced with a series of interpretations of life, common-sense understandings that are complex and difficult to separate from each other. The final product is a construction of these women's experiences as emergent themes which clarify for the reader issues of importance to Latinas.

## REFERENCES

Agar, M.H. (1980). The Professional Stranger: An Informal Introduction to Ethnography. New York: Academic Press.
Bogden, R.C., & Biklen, S.K. (1992). Qualitative Research for Education. Needham Heights, MA: Allyn and Bacon.
Goetz, J.P., & LeCompte, M.D. (1984). Ethnography and Qualitative Design in Educational Research. New York: Academic Press.
Jacob, E. (1987). Traditions of Qualitative Research: A Review. Review of Educational Research, 51, 1–50.
Lama Surya Das. (1997). Awakening the Buddha Within. New York: Broadway Books.
Locke, Don C. (1992). Increasing Multicultural Understanding. Newbury Park, CA: Sage.
Marshall, C., & Rossman, G. (1989). Designing Qualitative Research. Newbury Park, CA: Sage.
Merriam, S.B. (1988). The Case Study Research in Education. San Francisco: Jossey-Bass.
Miles, M.S., & Huberman, A.M. (1984). Qualitative Data Analysis: A Sourcebook of New Methods. Beverly Hills, CA: Sage.
Schatzman, L., & Strauss, A. (1973). Field Research: Strategies for a Natural Sociology. Englewood Cliffs, NJ: Prentice-Hall.
Spradley, James P. 1980. Participant Observation. Macalester College: Holt, Rinehart, and Winston, Inc.

Tesch, R. 1989. Textbase Alpha User's Manual. Qualitative Research Management. Desert Hot Springs, CA.

Van Manen, M. (1990). Researching Lived Experience: Human Service for an Action Sensitive Pedagogy. New York: The State University of New York Press.

Watson, L.C., & Watson-Franke, M.B. (1985). Interpreting Life Histories. New Brunswick, NJ: Rutgers University Press.

# CHAPTER 4

# Las Historias

F OR SEVERAL YEARS, I HAVE ASKED MYSELF, "WHY ARE LATINAS' LIVES IMPORTANT TO me?" The most obvious reason has been that I am a Latina. My search for importance in my life has led me to tell the stories of other Latina women. It's only natural to see your life in other people's lives. So in some ways, my search for self began by listening to others. Hearing other women speak of their families of origin, the culture and the rituals regarding being female in Mexican households, and how they relate to the world outside of the culture inspired me to ask more questions. What is striking to me is the staying presence of our culture. I have been in several conversations with non-Latinos who evoke great pride as just being an "American," no hyphenated names for them. These women on the contrary are very proud to use two names, sometimes three to remember their ethnic pride. These ethnic affirmations should not be divisive but often from those who show discomfort, they are. Consciously and unconsciously, the goal here is to affirm all Latinas who choose to empower themselves by proudly identifying with their ethnic background. Even though many women interviewed were acculturated to mainstream American society there were still special references that remain. There is a special language that Latinas speak even when not verbalized that evokes great feelings within us.

I was fortunate enough to be able to make a presentation at a national conference regarding my dissertation research with some Latinas who were my informants in New Orleans in June, 1993. The people who attended our session, many of them Latinas and Latinos, nodded vigorously while the women were discussing their families. The tears of these women evoked tears from the audience as well. I remember one woman in the audience saying she felt she was at a Twelve Step meeting for AA, it was so cathartic for her! What I felt when I heard statements like these is how unheard many of these Latina women feel, not only on the panel but in the audience. These voices are what compels me to write their stories.

Many women throughout their interviews looked at me and said, "You know what I mean." There is an interconnectedness between these women and me that reaches far beyond words. One of the women, Ramona, said it's "souls talking to each other." After the interviews these women asked a common question, "Can you tell me what the other women said?" Again, I felt this sense of not knowing who we are as a group of Latinas. We don't know each other and there is so much to discuss.

Why then are these life histories, which are so personal, perhaps depersonalized in the written form? Watson (1985) states "there is nothing so strange and at the same time so demanding as the written word. Writing involves self alienation . . . this task is accomplished by bridging the text back into the living presence of conversation, whose fundamental procedure is always question and answer, that is writing first be changed back into speech and meaning" (p. 44). I feel protective when interpreting these Latinas' life stories. In life histories, the quest is for the investigator to not only relate the informant's story, but to understand what is the motivating thrust for the investigator. According to Watson (1985), the hermeneutical perspective incorporates reflexivity (reflection) as an essential element in an interpretive framework (p. 14). The investigator must understand her own epistemological assumptions regarding the text. My interpretation is that telling these women's stories will evoke powerful feelings in other Latinas whose voices have not been heard and perhaps empower them in some ways to tell their own stories. Also it will help non-Latinos from diverse fields, whether academic, social services, or education, understand women from Latino culture.

One of the cardinal tenets of hermeneutics is that when we interpret and understand a text, like a life history, we see it in both unitary fashion as a whole and in terms of the parts that make it up. We cannot understand the whole without the parts except in reference to the whole. The construction of the thematic relationship of parts to the whole is one of the most important meanings of the hermeneutical circle (Gusdorf 1980; Van Manen 1990; Watson 1985). These women's stories are individually unique, yet when seen as a group of Latina women telling their stories, one can see certain patterns emerging that coexist in their lives as they connect to the culture.

For example, regarding work, many if not all of the women were dedicated and committed to helping people in the Latino community. They are involved in their communities by serving on boards, working in social service agencies which serve Latino communities and overall involvement. Another tie that binds them are their collective feelings regarding education. There has been a persistent and strong myth that has created burdens in the Latino community which states that Latinos do not give high regard to education. The myth is dying a slow death because many of these women still are asked if this disregard for education is true. They believe they have a mission to fulfill through education and all of them have continued with advanced education after high school or show a sincere desire to continue.

Therefore, we must attempt to understand Latinas lives through their perception of the culture that they've been raised in and understand. Hearing these Latinas speak of their lives with regard to their family, the culture, and success, ensures the respect that their voices deserve. Many of the women asked me why I feel that their life story is interesting or important. It occurred to me at these times that the women weren't asked often enough about their lives. It was both sad and exciting to feel that I could do something to help them feel validated by telling their stories. Of course there are differences among Latina women, but the similarities are what unite the strengths of Latinas which unfortunately many of us do not understand or even know exist.

The presentation of these life histories are fashioned in a narrative form keeping true to the authentic voices of the women. They discuss their lives with attention given to family, education, the Latino culture, success and the future. The names used are not the women's real names. Protecting their anonymity was crucial to them in order to speak freely about themselves and their families. Following this section will be a qualitative analysis which features an examination of dominant themes and patterns which have emerged overall in these women's life histories. The stories are timeless.

## I: EL CUENTO DE RAMONA

### "Indigenous Perspectives"

Ramona is 37 years old. She was born and raised in the Midwest. She is an assistant director for a shelter for homeless people. Ramona's home was welcoming with its pastel colors of peach and cream, mixed with dark forest greens and rich dark wood. We made ourselves comfortable on her over-stuffed furniture while her cat sat looking out through the window. She began her story with her parents. Her father is from Mexico and her mother was born in the United States. She reflects how her family traveled a lot. Her father she said, "took us to Mexico, what he considered to be the real Mexico", describing the "humble background" of her family:

> Something that I consider interesting and I think it's reflected in a lot of different ways, in the things that I do professionally as well as my personal interests is the strong indigenous bond. Our family came from humble backgrounds, they were not wealthy by any means, did not have a lot of formal education, but I think reflected some of the values that make our culture, our Mexican culture a strong one, that is the desire to learn, the desire to progress. A matter of personal progress, helping and maintaining a family reputation, those things are important.

Ramona is gratified by the artist in herself. She likes to play the piano and has taken ballet. She stated that movement to dance is important. An important visual sight was to look at these Latinas' homes. Many of them decorated in the same color schemes with natural woodwork being prominent. Ramona said this about her home, "Artistically, another way I express is with my home, when I decorate and put it together, that's a process. Looking at textures and creating a definite ambiance."

## "Mother's Radar"

Ramona spoke with pride in her family and culture, reminding herself of her family's strong bond to their cultural roots. She said that she was only beginning to realize the influence of her mother with the understanding that her father's influence was dominant which is typical of traditional patriarchal families. Reminiscing about her mother's ways of knowing elicited this response about intuition:

> One thing that I always have known about my mother is that she had an intuitive ability that she called jokingly, "her mother radar". She knows things before they happen, and that was just kind of a regular natural expected part of our upbringing.

Another natural and influential piece to Ramona's upbringing was the art of folk healing. She said that her family was exposed to traditional Western medicine, but her family was comfortable as well "looking through the eyes of a folk healer". She spoke of her grandmother who used the folk healer's methods of treating maladies. She also said that her grandmother felt that education was not only necessary but attainable. It wasn't a formal education only, but "character development, development of culture, those things were important and she knew about them." Memories of Ramona's grandmother as told by her mother and aunt, seemed to inspire Ramona to learn about folk healing and seeing the world in an integrated sense. As she spoke there was a strong feeling that Ramona was following in the footsteps of her grandmother in this respect. Ramona worked for a social service agency where not only the art of the folk healing blossomed, but a sense of understanding about where she saw herself as a folk healer:

> A real interesting awakening started to happen when I was at the Center. I started to listen to clients and it was a reinforcement for myself, having been socialized in the Anglo dominant society, I had realized what the core part of me had been denied and oppressed. Being exposed to the clients on a regular basis, I've seen more universal things about what being a Latino was.

## "Expression of the Soul"

Ramona explained this sense of "heightened awareness" seems to come from similar economic barriers. She said that being sensitive and accepting of these feelings is very important. Ramona spoke of this "intuitive inspiration" as something that she believed was much "older" in presence. Something that guided her toward the "feeling" approach even though a rational problem-solving attempt to the situation may have been more logical.

Ramona is a professional woman whose career choices have led her to a wide variety of positions. She speaks to community and professional groups about Latino families and considers herself a counselor. She said that she is impressed about the "universal themes" that indigenous cultures maintain. She spoke with a Native American once and was amazed that point after point they agreed on what approaches to take when working with Latino and Native American families, all without prior knowledge of each others presentations. The feeling that Ramona had regarding this event was very special:

> I'm looking at it very seriously because I notice that among indigenous populations, there are of course differences but I am also seeing some themes that I would call universal because there is truth for people who lived thousands of years ago and people who are living on opposite sides, thousands of miles apart. They are living their lives based on central values and central themes that are as true as they are for different groups even though they are separated and don't communicate usually. I think that speaks to a lot of the strengths of the culture and that's something that I'm beginning to realize now, realizing in myself and collectively looking at the culture especially when I do comparative sorts of presentations and analysis of my culture, the Latino culture. I guess that's what people refer to when they say eclectic, it's integrated, not just here is this piece, but how does it relate? This is how I see its importance and how it fits, the integrated, the indigenous perspective, which tends to be the big picture, the universal, yes I see the whole, but I also see the relationships.

She recalled an episode in her early life (age nine) which indicated what she later explained as "envisioning." She was in a daydream when she exclaimed to her older sister, "When I grow up, I want to be a psychologist!" Quickly, she remembers being told that being a psychologist would take too long in school and she felt somewhat discouraged:

> Inwardly, I now realize that I never abandoned that call to understanding the nature of the human psyche, never abandoned the call to understand what healing is, what wholeness is because those are very much a part of my life, an undeniable part of my life, an expression of my soul.

Ramona's refined talent of "seeing the bigger picture" has led her into in-depth discoveries regarding self-actualization. Ramona has a rich and deep understanding of herself and how she relates to others that may be described as altruism or according to Maslow (1968), a high degree of self-actualization:

> I envision something and I see its possibilities for coming into the physical reality. I can envision words being the same way, being very visual. There's a high integration of feeling to the point where I can now distinguish very subtle things just by feeling them. That's all part of the vision; it's not a static vision, it's a moving vision.

## "Searching and Searching"

Ramona's educational experiences were diverse. She attended public schools first through sixth grades and then went to Catholic schools for the remainder of her education. Ramona knew when she was in the eighth grade that she would be attending college and that a college education had been a strong family value. Initiating the choice herself, she selected an all girls' Catholic high school known for its college preparatory classes. This era for Ramona as she recalled, was particularly enlightening later in her life with respect to her growing awareness about spirituality and religion. She stated that at age 16 she began to feel that some of the answers that she received in religion classes weren't giving her what she needed:

> Something was stirring and asking me to look deeper. I went through a period that lasted several years, through the first year after high school, just kind of searching and searching.

Ramona commented on competition, "I'm not competitive, when I compete, it's with my own standards, not with other people. When I achieve something, it's because I feel good about achieving, so that's more internal." The themes of spirituality and its relationship to indigenous strengths supported Ramona's feeling about competitiveness and cooperation. She suggested that in terms of indigenous thinking, it is important not to compare oneself to people but to recognize that everybody has their experiences. A critical commonality among mostly all the Latina women was their commitment to helping others. Ramona's world-view regarding "respeto" (respect) toward others' values and feelings is prominent throughout her life.

## "Encountering the Soul"

Spirituality to Ramona was not limited only to Catholicism. Actually her search for deeper meaning led her to meet someone from New York who spoke of the teachings of "Gnosticism". Ramona said that Gnosticism literally translated means knowledge, "someone who seeks knowledge, wisdom, understanding the truth, ultimately what Gnostic seeks is universal truth." Maintaining her cultural perspective, Ramona stated that adhering to Gnosticism while individualized, did not lose sight of the indigenous roots of Latino culture.

> In the indigenous culture, people are encouraged to speak their own vision, so the one isn't done to the exclusion of the other, but the two are integrated. Whereas in dominant Anglo society, individualism is often the value, value pursuing distancing yourself from the family, whereas in the indigenous those two paths are integrated.

Ramona spoke of returning to graduate school. She has reservations about graduate school because the process is more on the traditional practice of education. She felt that much of what she would be taught would "go totally against the grain" of what she had learned about healing through indigenous ways. There was a sense of conflict about how to bring these two worlds together, the professional counseling program with credentials along with the natural and spiritual gift that Ramona possessed:

> I'm looking for a way to study at the master's level and justify in the minds of other people what I know that I know, making a bridge between two worlds. In a sense the agony is just as profound now as when I was searching for a bachelor's program, because any time you encounter the soul directly it is never a comfortable experience, never an easy experience.

Directly in touch with her spirituality, Ramona spoke also of "fate." She stated that fate can be either a conscious or unconscious effort on the part of the person. She called it a "vision" and a person will move along in life based on this vision:

> Kind of like moving within this sea of energy on a path, and each path is different, you can see where the path is very necessary and represents those things which the soul is seeking for its' life experiences. I see this nourishment, this magnetized nourishment, and so for me that's what fate is, it's magnetizing things to you.

Taken a step further, Ramona discussed how the supernatural is a natural part of the Latino culture, "that's a real part of our Latino experience is to be closer to what's considered supernatural, but actually what I think is little or unknown facts about what is very natural and nothing strange or unusual, magic or hocus pocus." She feels that belief in the supernatural goes across Latino subgroups (Puerto Ricans and Cubans) as well as all socioeconomic levels. There are voices to be guided by, according to Ramona, but unfortunately in this society hearing voices causes others to be alarmed:

It's a joke but I don't appreciate it as a joke, but I appreciate it as something very true of the dominant culture, the quote is, "when we talk to God, it's called prayer, but when God answers, it's called schizophrenia". A joke I don't appreciate but it does point out hearing voices is simply not considered as an option that is healthy in the dominant culture.

Ramona's thoughtful perspectives on success again illuminated her visions. Consistent with the pattern of helping others, Ramona's feelings about success were described as, "envisioning and embracing something deep in your core and joining on that deep level to "stimulate others." Speaking with Ramona about her life felt like "listening to the voice of wisdom". She's a very remarkable woman.

## II: EL CUENTO DE CARMEN

### "The Hard Route"

Carmen is 32 years old. She is a full time student and works in the mental health field. She was born in the south but has spent a lot of her adult life in the Midwest.

I sat with Carmen in her living room surrounded by deep dark woodwork, a lovely old fireplace and the sun shining through her east windows. I noticed on the table a bowl of rocks or gemstones which took me by surprise because in some of the other Latinas' homes, they also had bowls filled with rocks. Carmen began by telling me that she loved school in the elementary grades but started to have difficulty around third grade. It wasn't that the material was difficult, she still received B's and C's without much effort but it was "just downhill." Carmen stated that at times family life consisted of inappropriate or misdirected anger, "It seemed like nothing I did was good enough. When I did well in school I don't remember being praised. When I did poorly in school I do remember being criticized for that." Carmen continued to have difficulty in school and started to join more rebellious groups. She said, "I kind of went that route hard and heavy for throughout my early adult years until about four and a half years ago, I got into recovery as I was addicted to drugs and alcohol."

Carmen said that her parents were strict and that often the responsibility of "keeping things in line" fell on her and her older sister. Carmen said when her father was away from the home, her mother was much more lenient with the children, "I mean all the kids, we were just really happy because we could have some freedom and it was really much more relaxed around the house. We could breathe and be ourselves."

When asked about her mother, Carmen recalled that her mother had a difficult life. Her mother had died when she was young and she had her first child at a very young age. Her marriage offered her no support so she divorced Carmen's father. Throughout this conversation regarding her mother, Carmen showed support for her mother, "When I was about age 12 my mother became very religious and then she changed, she became a totally different person. She became real calm and loving, the kind of mom that we would all like to have."

Her mother has had more difficult times but Carmen feels that she is in a position now to be more understanding toward her mother. Throughout many of these interviews there have been turning points in each woman's life that has helped her to understand the bigger picture. In Carmen's life, the turning point seems to have been her own recovery program. Carmen is just beginning to understand the effects of some of the more harmful voices of her past:

> I knew that with all the messages that I grew up with I knew that I didn't like myself. I interpreted from my father that because I was Mexican I was no good and I was never going to make it in this world and my best bet, the only way I was going to make it was to tell people I was not Mexican, but if they asked, to tell them that I was white and if they pushed the issue to tell them that I was Spanish because Spanish was not as bad as Mexican. I was criticized real harshly when I got dark from being in the sun. He just made it real clear to us that Mexican was a very bad thing and if that was ever known to people then they would know how worthless and lazy, stupid and fat and ugly and all those things that were worse.

## "The Faith"

Carmen feels that now she has a greater understanding of herself and that working through these old voices, she recognizes that they are "false messages." Carmen stated that she tried very hard to disprove these messages and continues to find the balance in a healthy way, "but I guess today, I'm invalidating all those messages and that is real hopeful." Carmen firmly believed that she "wasn't going to grow up, I really did not think I would make it to age 30," she is now 32.

Even though Carmen felt she didn't fulfill her potential as a child in her early education, as an adult she believes this:

> I love to learn and now the way I look at it is that I had a lot of doors closed for me when I was very young because I was told that I was stupid and I believed it. When I was at a community college, I had my first instructor tell me that she thought I had a lot of potential and she hoped I would go on to pursue not only a bachelor's degree but a master's degree and that blew me away. I mean I just fell over and I felt so good. I came home and cried. How could somebody actually think that of me when I was still feeling, a little bit more self-esteem than an inch high.

As Carmen continued her education, more instructors advised her to continue on with her Ph.D. Carmen said at times the educational tasks are difficult and long, and then she remembers "it is the faith that other people had in me" that keeps her going.

Carmen's professional goals include being a professional counselor. When she spoke of success she said that she believes success is a person doing what they want to be doing and they feel good about it. Success also includes her healthy recovery program, "I mean recovery is a process of a new way of living, a new way of life." When Ramona spoke of the "path of the soul" as being a difficult journey, Carmen relates to this journey in a similar way:

> Working on all my defects of character means for me to make conscious efforts to improve the things about myself that I don't like. If I don't like that I'm being real critical then I need to work on that. If I don't like that I'm being real dishonest, I need to work on that. That's a big part of the program, honesty. You have to be honest with yourself, honest with other people, honesty is crucially important. So recovery is not just a part of my life, it is my life.

## "Enjoying the Journey"

Carmen's attention to her spirituality is integrated with her recovery. Her faith in her "higher power" is a God that is loving and supportive, "the humorous type that lets me be a person and lets me be me." Carmen depends on her higher power to help her through difficult times:

> My higher power works through other people. I will give you an example, it was my first class at this university and I took a test along with 97 other students. Looking at my test results, I scored a 96, but what really blew me away was that I ranked in the 98 percentile! That meant I was practically at the top of my class, you know two away from the top. I just sat there looking at all these scores for probably ten minutes, I'd walk away, then come back, thinking perhaps I was dreaming or that somebody was playing a trick on me. Three days later I was upset and crying, I still could not believe that I could be placed with those students. My friend bought me a sympathy card that read, 'sorry about your loss, the loss of the belief that you are stupid.' When I was crying it was like conflicting, on the one hand I am seeing I cannot be stupid if I scored that high and still feel stupid! When I saw the actual test, I believed my score. I went home and read my sympathy card and cracked up.

As far as future plans, Carmen intends to finish her undergraduate degree and then continue with a master's program. She'd like to be an inpatient counselor because she said, "you know people (in inpatient programs) are really in worse shape, those are the kind of people that I'd like to work with first." She is also interested in education and perhaps in teaching someday. Carmen stated that she'd like to develop an inpatient program for prisoners as well. When I asked how she came to think of herself working with prisoners, she replied:

> I really have a desire to work with those people because they are like me, in that, I also felt that I could never be successful. I also felt that the only way that I was going to make it was to rob, steal, and I felt that the world owed me. I have changed a lot in those ways so I know that there is hope for that population. I am such a different person today than what I used to be and it feels good . . . to hear it coming from me. I am definitely on the right path and enjoying the journey because like they say if you don't enjoy the journey, you are not going to enjoy it when you get there, so today I am enjoying the journey.

After difficult situations in her life, Carmen has been able to discover the strengths that she possesses. As Ramona wanted to be a "bridge to reach out to people," Carmen also wants to help others. She stated it so eloquently when she said in others she sees herself, she doesn't want them to give up. Carmen will help others because she is discovering her inner strengths and has become empowered.

## III: EL CUENTO DE GLORIA

### "I Found a Part of Myself"

Gloria is 28 years old. She is a part time student and works for a large social service agency. Gloria's home is decorated for comfort, overstuffed furniture and the entertainment center is in a prominent place which led me to believe that music is important to Gloria's family. As in some others' homes, the woodwork was all natural. It was interesting to hear Gloria start by saying, "I'm Mexican. I'm originally from Mexico City, born in Mexico City, raised here." She works at a social service agency and plans to continue her education in the helping professions:

> First my family is my priority but secondly close to first, is my education and then my work at the Center. I know things will change because of my education and because I want to work with families more, life revolves around the Center.

When I asked Gloria what "life revolves around the Center" meant, she replied:

> I went to Catholic schools where there were three or four minority students out of 200 students in my class. There really wasn't a sense of identity, I felt like I didn't know who I was, even though my fam-

ily was traditional. I didn't see a lot of other Mexican faces at my high school. I think because of that experience and the isolation that I felt when I was in high school, the Center seems special to me because I found a part of myself. I'm seeing with other young women, especially, the effect that I can have on their lives, by just being a part of their lives. That's important to me right now. They're like an extension of my family because I know the community. I know a lot of students and their families and I feel a connection much more than a counselor relationship. I feel a connection with the community.

Gloria's feeling is that the people she works with also experience similar feelings that she has regarding "living in two cultures." She comments on the constant struggle within oneself that "sometimes only people who live it, understand it." While others try to understand, their understanding may be in a different way.

## "Just Like a Cycle"

Gloria is very proud of her family. All of her siblings have finished high school and have continued becoming professionals. It is interesting again to shed attention toward the helping professions and how these Latinas are drawn toward helping others. Gloria's siblings (all females) are nurses, teachers and social workers. She said that graduating from high school was an expectation that her parents had and then in a pattern, "we graduated, then got married, and then we went back to school (college), which is kind of weird, kind of different."

Gloria definitely feels a deep attachment to being born in Mexico, she stated that it has "given me more of an identity." When her parents were settling in the United States she said they didn't quite know what to ask, they were first generation:

> Both my parents just kind of accept things because we were foreigners here in the United States. That sense of identity helped me towards the opportunity I have now because it was a strong base for me to know where I came from and know who my grandparents were, to visit them and know the language, just know the traditions and everything. That was a base for me to develop more in terms of opportunities.

It is apparent that Gloria's parents provided the inspiration for Gloria. Gloria stated that her parents suffered from discrimination, but they tried to protect the children. She said now she cries whenever she hears about these events because she never thought it could happen. When I asked her what she would do differently with her daughter regarding discussions about discrimination, she said:

Just that other people see differences as maybe bad, but other people sometimes see cultures or different colors as being something negative. Everyone is different, but it's not better nor worse, it's just different. The reality is that people do see people that are different in a negative way. You just need to be aware of it.

Gloria's family of origin is quite close and they gather together weekly to have dinner or celebrate birthdays. Now her nephews are old enough to work with her father who she thinks is passing on some tradition through his stories:

So the kids are working with my Dad this summer and I think that's special because you know Dad tells stories a lot and he talks about how things were when he was growing up. What he didn't have being poor and humble.

Gloria spoke of the visits to Mexico to visit her grandparents. She said that her grandparents were poor, but they were happy. Her grandfather would make tortillas and chile and they would just eat, "it wouldn't be so much what we had, it would be just the relationship that we'd have with each other." Parents of any culture will try and do the best for their children out of love. Gloria said that traveling back to Mexico with her parents each year helps her to remember this love that her parents had toward the children:

My parents sacrificed those relationships with their parents and brothers and sisters. That sacrifice was special because the detachment from their families was because of us. Knowing that Mom and Dad came to this country to give us a better life.

For many of these Latinas being a role model is very important. Many of the women do not even consider themselves role models. When I talked with Gloria about this subject, it was clear that she had thought about her role:

I see myself when I look at some of the young girls there. I see myself because I remember being in some dysfunctional relationships or not knowing what I wanted to do. I feel that I've grown since then and so I hope to maybe be an example for them. I'll probably keep going hopefully, and then they will come in and take over and I see it's just like a cycle. You know my nieces and nephews probably will be sitting in those chairs and they'll be talking to them, hopefully that's the way it will happen. Some of the people that I'm working with now, will be in the position that I'm in and then we'll be in a position to help others. Hopefully I'll be able to help them.

When I asked Gloria what she thinks about when she thinks of God, she replied that she thought of her grandparents and how religious they were. She said she hasn't come to terms with death but she knows there is contentment, "that's what I hear death is like." Gloria said in Spanish there are terms for accepting death, "mande a Dios, God willing, if God wills it, then it will be." The issue of death was interpreted in similar ways amongst the women. In some families, death was discussed in a very humorous way, with Gloria she is still uncomfortable with the thought.

Gloria views success as family oriented and is concerned with how the whole family benefits by her success. She credits her family for her success:

> Success is just being happy, being happy with what I do. I see me not having a lot of money now but I know reality is, I do want a good job. But I think success means more to me, happiness and being comfortable with my family and with my children. Just being able to, maybe help my mom and dad. I feel great that my baby is so smart and that to me is success. Seeing my nieces and nephews look up to me, I guess being successful is just being in relationships that are important to me. Being in school and able to wear different hats that are new, being a mother, a wife, a student, a teacher, a sister, a friend, that's what makes me happy.

Gloria became so involved in hearing herself speak about what makes her feel successful, that she didn't want to stop talking, she told me, "I want to keep talking!" She reiterated that success really meant having relationships with others that were meaningful. She stated that she really enjoys being around older people and thought maybe this was "her calling." She recalled visiting her husband's grandfather in Mexico the first year after they were married:

> I remember meeting his grandfather, this man impressed me so much, it wasn't anything he did, it was just his presence. He was probably in his 80's. He just accepted me, I felt like I knew him a long time. There was something about his knowledge, about respecting him because he was so old, the "bendicion" (blessing) is something that I'll always remember. Everybody kind of knelt down when he gave the bendicion (blessing). That was a special time for me, I can't explain it. It bought back memories for me of when I was a little girl visiting my grandparents who blessed me. A few weeks later I was back at work and a colleague said to me, "Don't you give your daughter the bendicion"? It's like God, I'm a parent now, I can do that, and so I will.

Gloria's family's past (including husband's family) is helping her shape her present and future for her family. She is not forgetting the lessons of her family. She said that her calling to work with the elderly may come from her grandmother's words of treating the elderly with respect because someday you will be old and someone will treat you kindly as well. Gloria lives her life treating others with respect and the vision that she sees of herself is a positive one.

## IV: EL CUENTO DE CAROLINA

### "The Responsible One"

Carolina is 33 years old. She was born in a southern state but has grown up in the Midwest. She works for a large school district where she works with youth. She considers herself a helping professional.

Carolina's home had the soft textures of mauve and blue with a lot of gold ornaments on the walls. Some of these pieces Carolina made herself. The furniture pieces were a deep dark wood like mahogany or cherry wood. Carolina began by saying that she's always been a little shy. She said that growing up in a strict family there wasn't really an opportunity to speak. She said this about being the oldest:

> Being the oldest, I was taught to be the responsible one, and not only the oldest child in my family, but the oldest grandchild. So I always thought of myself as the experiment child. It's harder for the oldest to get away with things. Lots of times I was blamed for things that my siblings did, because I should have known better.

Carolina thought about the roles that she had as a young female growing up in her home. She remembered working alongside her mother in the kitchen and felt that it was because she was the oldest. Now she thinks about her siblings playing outside, while she was inside doing some work, "I used to think that because I was the oldest but now I think it was also because I'm female. I think it's a cultural thing because that's what I saw in my extended family too."

There was an incident that Carolina recalled where her mother took charge of the situation. A teacher was mispronouncing her name. One day, Carolina said the principal came and talked with the teacher, her mother was there. This event is important to Carolina, she said, "People always ask now, "when did you first realize that you were different? And that's probably when I first realized it."

Carolina reminisced about her father a lot. She commented that her mother often would tell how much like her dad she was; they both want to be right! It appeared to me that the role model for Carolina was her father:

> I also learn a lot from my dad. In other ways we're alike, we're interested in the same kind of things, you know, like social issues. I remember dad talking about Cesar Chavez and we boycotted the grapes and lettuce. When I was little, I really didn't care about those things but now I like knowing about these things. I know why my

dad is the way he is sometimes and his behavior. I realize where he's coming from now and I feel good about that.

## "Connected to Somebody"

Even though Carolina was very shy, she was involved in a mariachi group when she was young. She recalled how she made her choice to play in the mariachi, "The dancers had to go on stage and dance in front of everyone, so I thought the musicians didn't have to do that. But then I had this nice surprise first thing . . . I had to go on stage too!"

Carolina attended Catholic schools even though her father wanted her to attend public schools. She said her dad was right again:

> I was 14 years old and I didn't care about quality, but now I see what he was talking about. Here's one of the things that I didn't like. I was at a school that put us in different levels. From freshman to senior years, you were an "A", "B", "C", or "D" level. Well, "A" kids took French, trig, hard classes. It was really bad they way they did that to us. Everybody knew what everybody was because the school was so small. You knew who was a "C" and "B" student.

Carolina was deeply affected by this unfair treatment of dividing students according to skill level. She stated that she had many friends who were in different levels, so she never felt put down, yet she didn't appreciate the separation system.

Carolina had an interest in art and liked to draw still lives but another artistic interest is decorating. Ramona also enjoyed putting textures together and being an artist in her home, "You know, putting colors together, that's probably why I like to do makeup, because it seems artistic to me, fun to put colors together, to blend."

## "The Next Step"

We talked about how she decided to go to college. Education has always been an important value in Carolina's family. Her father was able to take a few college courses but Carolina is the first in her family of origin to work toward a master's degree. There seemed to be a lot of male role models that Carolina was listening to, to learn more about what she should do. She said that a teacher in high school was disappointed that she didn't attend college right after high school. Carolina said that she saw her just recently and felt this way:

> It felt good to see her and say, "see, I did go and now I'm in my master's program." I didn't really say that to her, but I was thinking it and I wanted her to know what I was doing. Just that I know I did it, because I kept saying I knew I would, but nobody believed me.

Carolina had some difficulty with her first choice in business. She persevered through many of the classes, but finally decided this "wasn't what I wanted." She perused through an academic catalog and found a discipline that helped others. This appealed to her and so she started the program. Her grade point average improved as an undergraduate and now she is in her graduate program.

Carolina recalled an event that is rather humorous in one sense but shows part of the traditional Mexican family rules in another sense:

> I would take the bus everywhere, when mom and dad got another car, they would let me drive the older one, then I was never home. My dad would get mad and I remember him saying something about always running around or not at home. I'd think to myself, that's why I got my license so that I wouldn't have to be home all the time.

It wasn't that Carolina did like being home, but she needed to be more independent and her parents seemed to have a little difficulty adjusting to her growing independence. Carolina found out about a job opening working with young people in the Latino community shortly after she graduated with her bachelor's degree. At first she didn't feel she was qualified and she had some doubts about the job. She interviewed though and was selected for the position. This opportunity proved to be a turning point for her in her career and personal life:

> At first I was a little intimidated by these young people. They were a little rough, but once I got to know them, I really liked them a lot. I always tell this to people, that I never really felt my culture. I thought I was the same as everyone else and I didn't think my family was traditional in the Mexican culture until I started working with these other Latinos, especially Latinas. When the girls would tell me some things about their problems at home and maybe like role expectations, then I realized my family was more traditional than I thought. I started feeling like I could relate more to somebody. Now, I was starting to feel like I was connected to somebody and there is some good that I can do.

The feeling of being connected seems to be an important issue in many of these Latinas' personal and professional lives. Carolina commented also about the family like atmosphere of the agency that she worked for:

> Because we were all Latinos, I never had that before. It seemed so much fun to be at work and hear all the Spanish and people making jokes and you knew what they were talking about. You know, even though I don't know that much Spanish I could lots of times understand things that people were saying. Just the way we were able to relate to each other was so much fun that I've never had before. You

can have that with other people of color to an extent, but it's so different with your own. You know, I guess, I never realized what difference there was before. Right now at work, I can get along with people but don't feel really as close. I don't feel the same closeness that I did, not like family, even though people at work will say that. They say they feel like family and maybe they do with each other, but I don't feel that way with them.

Carolina seems to be very adaptable in her life. She has been flexible as far as work and education. Even though it has been difficult and tiresome for her to balance these two events, she has persevered throughout it all. Carolina's career took a turn in her life that again would shed more light on her own family's patterns. She started working in a substance abuse program. She really didn't know that much about substance abuse but she taught herself a lot about the dynamics of it. She also took classes in chemical dependency:

I'm glad that we had to take those classes. I realized that I had more experience in substance abuse than I thought, because that's when I realized that my family was dysfunctional. It was around this time that my mom finally admitted that my grandpa was an alcoholic, and I had never realized it. I started to understand that many of my family members had alcohol problems.

Carolina admitted that being a role model for other Latinos was gratifying for her. She stated that she does a lot of guest speaking in classes and she enjoys giving people accurate information about Latinos:

Many people have stereotypes and I'm able to tell them about our background a little bit so that they don't stereotype. We talk about the good and the bad stereotypes and how exposing different cultures to each other is good. I can show others (Latinos) that they can be independent. They can pretty much do what they want as far as careers and education. I think that they can maintain the culture and still take things from the dominant society too. See, for me, independence is important. I know in some Latino families, independence is not encouraged because the family fears the children will pull away from the culture. I can still hold on to the culture and be independent at the same time.

Carolina is more of a shy person, so when I asked her how she speaks in front of large groups of people, she replied that it takes some getting used to. She also said that speaking about the Latino culture was something that she felt comfortable with, but there have been times when she's been directly challenged about her interpretation of the culture:

> One time a Chicano teacher got real angry, actually she was a
> Mexican teacher from Mexico and she didn't identify with a thing
> that I said. She would say, "That's not the way we are and where did
> you get your information?" She was mad! I recall that she was light
> skinned with dark hair and I didn't know she was Mexican. I was talk-
> ing about how some Latinos are more present time oriented than
> future time oriented and she just raised her hand and said, "Where do
> you get all your information? Because none of that's right." My heart
> was just pounding in front of all these people but I was really calm
> and I explained to her that I am speaking from my own perspective
> and from my experiences of working with families. She held her book
> in front of her face talking to her classmate while I continued to talk.
> I could see that she was really angry.

Knowing that Carolina is shy, I was curious about how she handled this
particular incident in front of all these people. She said that she uses humor
a lot in her discussions if she can. She feels at times that she's violating some
family secret and said that perhaps her family wouldn't appreciate all that
she says, but she feels that teaching others about the culture is important and
hopes that they would understand.

When Carolina identified herself as a Chicana I asked why she used this
ethnic identification term. She called it an "ethnic conscious term which
means that she's proud to be of Mexican descent and committed to her heritage." She felt that utilizing this term helped her take the next step toward
self-affirmation because the term is not used that often.

Carolina shared a lot about her feelings toward her father. Carolina has
much respect for him and his life experiences. He originally is from an area
of the country where there are a lot of Mexicans and he discussed his fears
about the police while he was growing up there and about discrimination.
Carolina said she never recalled a time when her dad was disrespectful to
other people, Anglos, Blacks or anybody else:

> You know he was always bringing people in or trying to take care of
> people. And that has been an influence on me. Our whole family is
> like that, but I think dad has that commitment even though he was-
> n't able to go to college or be a professional, he deep down inside feels
> committed to helping people, especially other Mexicanos or
> Chicanos.

## "The Only One"

Carolina is attending graduate school. She stated that "it's fun and it's hard
and I love the classes a lot." She spoke of the quick changes though when students graduate. Some of the students that she connects with are ready to
move on and she feels a sense of loss and isolation. In addition to this feel-

ing is the sense that she's the "only Latina":

> The first day of our orientation I looked around and can remember
> only a few minorities. I don't really remember seeing any Latinos. I'm
> probably the only one and this is really disappointing. I really feel iso-
> lated and it just seems weird.

Carolina reflected on what her life will look like after two years. She hopes to
have her master's degree and also a child. She recalled a dream where she felt
pulled in many directions:

> I even dreamt about being torn, torn between . . . I think deep down,
> I'm traditional and even though sometimes I want to fight or reject
> those gender role expectations, I'm also comfortable with that. I want
> to be a mom and a wife and I do like to take care of my house. I don't
> think there's anything wrong with staying home with your kids. On
> the other hand, there are so many things that I would like to do as far
> as a career, so many things that I would like to accomplish but then,
> how do you do all that?

Carolina sees success as feeling good about what you've done, no matter
what it is. She remembered that her earlier school days as an undergraduate
were stressful but she persevered and obtained her undergraduate degree. She
said there was a professor that told her what do grades matter anyway? She
felt relieved when he told her this because part of her definition of success
means being able to use what she's learned. The grades are meaningless
unless you are able to use the knowledge gained through the classes and also
helping the community, "Something that's important to me is to contribute
to the community. So now the skills that I'm learning can be used in the
community."

Carolina's attitude toward her life and what goals she has attained
already shows her flexibility:

> Not that I'm being pessimistic but sometimes I think, what if I had to
> go back and be a waitress? At least I know how to do it. I don't think
> I'd be that devastated. It would be hard, but I know if I had to do it,
> I could. And you know, I feel more enriched and I think that's part of
> success too. Is that the right word?

When Carolina asked me if enriched was the right word, I smiled thinking
that if Carolina lost everything that she has worked for so diligently she
would rise to the challenge in a positive approach and begin all over again.

## V: EL CUENTO DE MARY

## *"This Is What I Am"*

Mary was born and raised in the Midwest. She is 29 years old and works for a social service agency, primarily with youth. She is the youngest child of five children. Mary commented that there are large age differences between her and her siblings. Her mother had Mary when she was 42 years old. She said that she comes from a very traditional family where her mother stayed at home with the children and her father worked, "My father worked at the packing house and before that was a migrant worker. He decided to move the family to this area and we've been here ever since."

Mary attended Catholic schools. As a matter of fact, the school was located next door to her house. She remembered her mother walking her next door and waiting when she got out of school. Mary said that her family was very supportive. Mary said that education was important to the family even though it wasn't verbalized:

> When I expressed an interest to go to college, my parents thought it would be a good idea. So I decided in about 10 minutes to be a dietician. I went away to college and lived on campus. It was my first time away from home.

At the time that Mary was going to college, she stated that all she thought about was making money and getting a good job to better her life. Mary began to explore her feelings about being a Latina in college:

> But at that time, I wasn't real in touch with my heritage or my identity as a Latino, Mexicana. You know I was really out of touch with that. I knew in vague sort of way that I was Mexican. Well, I knew that. But I didn't feel whatever that meant. I was very in touch with my American culture and I think it was easier for me to be a part of the American culture and feel more accepted into that because of the fact that I am lighter skinned and that brings up a lot of feelings within myself too. Because I was in the majority at college, I never shared or talked about the culture with my friends that I lived with in the dorm. I was the only woman of color now that I think about it. I wasn't involved with multicultural affairs then I was pretty much out of touch with it. I didn't really feel a sense of loss or not part of the American culture because I seemed to be accepted or maybe I was so naive that I didn't see maybe the non-acceptance.

This remembrance certainly brought up a lot of questions for Mary. She realized that her brother helped her a great deal to understand who she was:

> I was sitting in my parents' home and I don't know what prompted me, probably one of my brother's books, my oldest brother, who is

deceased now and did a lot of cultural family history. I started to think, okay Mom was born in Mexico and she grew up in the United States. I knew that my dad was born in the U.S. but then I got to thinking about my grandparents, both sets of grandparents were from Mexico and it just dawned on me, I am 100% Mexican, 100%. I guess it just stressed to me, this is what I am and I felt this enormous sense of loss because I had no idea. I feel like I am still searching and learning more about that. But at the time it was a total crisis for me because of this total awareness that I had no idea what that means.

## "Emotional Sobriety"

Mary felt that her home was traditional. Dad worked and made all the decisions and Mom was the nurturer and the caregiver at home. Mary stated that she didn't think she wanted a relationship like her parents:

> I'd like it to be more equal and I want it to be more a sharing of the decision-making processes of our home. But my parents are of a different generation so I'm sure that has a lot to do with it. It's taken a lot for me to accept that and still sometimes I don't understand.

Mary attributes her spirituality and faith to her mother. She recalls going to mass every Sunday, confession, receiving all the sacraments and observing holy days. She said her mother would say, "there was nothing in this world that was ever going to change her mind about Catholicism and her kids would be Catholic and devout." Mary also said her mother would say if anything, that's all she ever had in her life was her faith. Mary's faith is inspired by being Catholic but says she feels more spiritual than religious:

> I'd like to think that I find the spirituality within my religion. Being Catholic is very important to me but the rituals and the dogma I sometimes disagree with. Sometimes every decision I make I turn to the spirit to help me. You go to church on Sunday and then you work and I never thought about bringing spirituality or my faith into the workplace and that's changing for me now. I feel that I have this contact, this conscious contact. It's interesting. It's real interesting.

The concept of success to Mary included being independent. Mary felt that success meant having serenity and happiness in life in any position:

> I guess I feel like I'm a lot less controlling or have this perceived control over my future. What I think it should be and where I should be in the position and the status that should go along with that. That's not as important to me any more and I think, for awhile, it was. I have to be honest and say status and the power that goes along with

that was wrapped up in my definition of success. I remember coming home on the weekends and going to church and people would ask, how's school going? I'd feel real good about that and I was very proud of the fact that I was in college. But now I can look beyond all that and to me, it's a matter of being serene, having what I call "emotional sobriety." To me, that's success to know how to live in a healthy way, emotionally healthy as well as physically and spiritually. And before, I would kind of say that but I didn't really believe it.

Mary discussed how other friends see success as having a nice car, clothes and money. She said at one time she felt, "yeah, that's success," but now realizes it goes much deeper than that for her. She said that people asked her if she were afraid of success:

I don't know I think maybe in a way, I am. I am from the standpoint that my role model, my mother, gave me a very good example of how to run a home and how to be a good manager of house duties, which are important. But I never really had close to me, a professional woman role model. So when I think of success, I automatically think of the work world, the real world and that's when I do get fearful. My parents were blue-collar workers, hard workers. So now I feel like I'm kind of stepping into a different part of society. I don't know if that's right. It's like I get a little fearful because I'm not sure how I fit into all that.

## "What's Inside My Heart"

When Mary talked about her mother as a role model, it was enlightening to hear her response to being called a role model herself:

Oh wow! I guess I never really thought that I was a role model until last year. I'll talk freely about that a little bit. I'm in a recovery program. I'm recovering from substance abuse. I really feel that in the last year I've done a lot of serious work on those issues and now I feel like I probably could be (a role model). It's real hard for me to talk about that because I feel like I'm tooting my own horn and I don't like to do that. I think I feel comfortable saying that I am a role model to other women that may be dealing with the same type of issues and see how I've experienced those issues and come through it. In some way by my experience and strength and hope, then yeah, I guess I am a role model. But see it's real hard for me to say I am a role model.

Throughout this discourse I felt that Mary wasn't feeling very comfortable with being seen as a role model to others. I felt compelled to ask more questions about her uneasiness about this role:

I feel like I have to toot my horn coming up for this job opportunity and I am just not real good at that. I guess it has always been taught to me that you stay humble. Tooting your own horn, I feel like a lot of people can do that real well. I was raised with an attitude that you always do your best in everything that you do and good things will come to you. I'm still coming in touch with my talents, my creativity, and my confidence.

Mary thought the event that would inspire her confidence about being a role model would be learning more about the culture:

My journey into knowing who I am and part of that, a large part has to do with my culture. This is what I am. I am a Mexican woman and somehow I see that a lot of that will be brought into awareness and comfort when I have a better idea of what that means. What does it mean to be a Mexican woman in the United States of America, to be accepted as a productive worker but also to be loyal to what is dear to me and my customs and my traditions and my culture? I see myself in the future living in Mexico and that gives me a real good feeling. I get fearful and not very confident sometimes, like this job opportunity. I ask, can I do this, can I do this job? Maybe I can't, then I hear the old tapes in my head and I know from experience what I need to do is to go through the process, if it is meant to be I will be there.

Mary said that she is searching for her culture. She hopes that someday all the searching won't come from the outside looking for her culture but her sense of identity will come from the inside. What has helped Mary with this process is the opportunity to speak to some women who are going through substance abuse treatment. She has been asked on several occasions to speak to Latina women in recovery. The lead counselor has admitted that she doesn't know a lot about Latino culture. Mary stated that sharing is very important:

They nod their heads when they listen to what I'm saying. It's like, we know. The stories may be a little bit different but they're really not. I mean, we're all the same and the experiences may be different, but essentially the experiences are very, very similar. It's really eerie because these women are from different parts of the state, some from different parts of the country. It's real interesting to me how that works.

When I asked Mary if the strong commonality was the treatment aspect and not the cultural ties, she responded:

When I lived at a halfway house, I was the only Hispanic woman there. There was also a Native American woman but the rest were

Anglo. The Native American woman and I touched base a lot and I had to think it had a lot to do with culture. There was more of a feeling of knowing that she understood where I was coming from and she has some Mexican blood in her too. Her grandmother spoke Spanish so I'm sure she was, at least a little bit Mexican too. We all connected on the addictions that we were fighting, but the living experiences were different. When we shared, I understood her story, I mean it was a feeling of . . . it just fit. It just fit.

Her mother and father try their best to understand Mary's recovery program. Mary said that she would like her parents to support her and can accept their way of helping her. She spoke about her extended family and how close they all are. Mary recalled that some of her friends call them enmeshed, which Mary didn't agree with, "I begin to wonder about that, you know, am I enmeshed? I don't think so. I just think that's part of our cultural background, we are a close family."

Mary has some strong feelings regarding speaking Spanish. When she was small, her parents didn't speak Spanish in the home and Mary feels a little angry with this at times. She understands that her parents suffered from discrimination and through not speaking Spanish in the home, they felt they were giving her an edge:

I just want to say (to Mom and Dad), why didn't you speak Spanish when I was little? I mean, I know in my head why, you know. Mom and Dad went through a lot of discrimination and so did my grandparents. I think it's interesting how generations afterward still feel the effects of that in one way or another.

When Mary and I were ending this interview, I asked if there was anything else that she wanted to share. The topic became her spirituality and how the culture has played a major part in its endurance. She feels that learning more about her Indian roots are very important and Indian people are the most spiritual people that she's met. Learning more about her culture Mary states, is profound:

When I do participate in cultural events and speak to people that are sensitive to my culture, it's wonderful. It's like, I know this is where I need to be, or this makes sense. It's like another little piece to the puzzle that I'm putting into place. It's real profound. I feel like I'm not being very articulate as far as letting you know exactly what's inside my heart but that's kind of the way it is for me. I'm sure it's going to be a life long process. I kind of think that I'll reach 50 and I'll have all the answers. I'll know who I am and what I'm all about. That means, you know, to be a Mexican woman, but I don't think it's going to be that way, I think it's going to be a life long journey.

Mary is going through many transformational changes in her life, not only in her professional life but also in her personal journey to learn all she can about her culture. She has faith that someday she'll be older and understand all these questions she has today about what it means to be a Latina.

## VI: EL CUENTO DE LEORITA

### "The Culture Just Clashed"

Leorita is 37 years old. She works as a blue-collar worker in a manufacturing program. She is married and has four children. Leorita's home is brightly decorated in peach and cream colors. Her living room area was large and airy with gold ornaments and flowers on the table. Leorita began by describing the hardships that her mother especially suffered when she first came to the United States. Her mother didn't know the English language, she wasn't used to being away from her mother and the children were still too small to help her understand English. They returned to Mexico for awhile and Leorita attended first and second grades in Mexico. Now, all the family live in the same city, including Leorita's mother:

> No one's gone away. I can't imagine having any one of them away, at all. We lived in this part of the city that is considered the Mexicano barrio. Then we moved just a few blocks and I thought it was miles and miles away from my mom. That was really hard, so we bought a house on the same block where my mom lived. Then we bought this house and I finally got used to the idea that I live maybe a mile and a half away from my mom.

Leorita said that her mom and dad never pushed the family to go to school, but she's quick to state that she doesn't blame her mom and dad either. Her high school years were a little unsettled, she returned to Mexico during her sophomore year and stayed there for a couple of years. What Leorita didn't realize was that the credits she earned in school in Mexico didn't transfer to the U.S. schools:

> I never did go back. I don't know, like my husband told me, you don't have to go to everything that happens in school. I go, yes, I do, because my mom and dad never did. I just feel I have to do that for my kids. I have to push them. I have to push them to finish school, to go on to school, because my mom and dad were never there for me...but I don't blame them.

Leorita said that going to Mexico for awhile was an idea that her mom suggested. There were culture clashes between her father's interpretation of "boys and stuff" and what Leorita understood. She stayed with a family member in Mexico and went to school:

It was quite an experience and I'm glad I did it. I found out what it was all about, why my mom and dad were this way. And, you know I didn't understand them. When I moved there and lived there, I knew where they were coming from.

Leorita has young adult children of her own now and at times she feels that she is still trying to find the balances between cultures. Her children want to fit in with their friends in the United States:

I really feel like I don't have a culture. I feel like I'm caught in the middle. I don't agree with everything in the white culture, that's just not me. But yet I can't deal with just the plain Mexican culture either. So, I'm in the middle. You know, damned if you do and damned if you don't. You know, sometimes it's real hard.

Leorita discussed how she and her husband get together with other couples to do things. Their friends tell them that they're really into the Mexican culture, more so than the other couples. Leorita said that she felt it was important to her that the kids know who they are. Retaining and encouraging her children to speak Spanish is very important. Sometimes she feels discouraged when Mexican people don't speak Spanish:

That's just a sad feeling to me (not being able to speak Spanish). We push Spanish a lot. We go to Mexico once a year. I tell them (the children), be proud that you're Mexican. I think when I was raised, you didn't admit that you were Mexican.

Leorita really likes to be involved with her children, family, friends, and helping the community. She recalled a meeting that she had with the Board of Education. They wanted to know from her perspective how children viewed prejudice. She said that when she was in school, she tried her best to go unnoticed and not bring attention to herself. She admitted she would stay in the back in those days. Now she said children are seeing a lot more prejudice and feel they can stand up for themselves and be proud of who they are. Leorita felt adult role models contributed to the problem too:

I went to see a counselor once with my child. You know, the first thing that she said, was probably one of the first times I've felt, lady, who are you? She said that she thought it was my child's problem, she hadn't even met my child yet. She talked to me for fifteen minutes and said, I think maybe it's because your child's Hispanic. Your child is trying to fit in with the white people. I said don't tell me that. I know my kid and that is not the problem. You know that's the first time that I ever confronted somebody telling me that to my face. I told my husband that I couldn't believe that someone in her position would say that. She told me that she was from a small town and had never met a Mexican before. She's been one of the few persons that I've met in my life that's been so naive about what's going on around her.

## "I've Proved Myself"

Leorita talked about how her mother does things in different ways than herself. For example her mother will tell Leorita to do certain things for her husband. Leorita has a difficult time with these suggestions and has encouraged her mother not to do so much for her father:

> Why should I let him put me down like that? Why should I do everything? In a way, I guess I admire her for sticking it out, I mean life, the way it is with her and dad. I learned early in my marriage life, hey they're happy. Who am I to judge them? It's so hard for me to see her being bossed around by my dad. But I think, what gets me over there (to her parents' house) is love, you know. I guess it is. When we get together as friends, we talk about this (serving the men) and I didn't do it for a long time. I am not about to serve my husband, I say, "You serve yourself, you want to eat, you serve yourself." And now, you know, it's like okay I've proven that I don't have to, and now I will. No big deal, if he comes in and says, "You guys ready to eat? Well, go get me a plate." No big deal, it's not like he's bossing me. But for years, I would not do that. I would take it the other way, go get me a plate. I'd say, "Go get it yourself." I've proved myself and I'm not going to be bossed around.

Leorita finds it difficult at times to be caught between cultures, especially while she and her husband are raising their children. Her second oldest child is dating and would like to bring the girlfriend over to the house. Leorita and her husband agree that it's not permissible. Her son reacts to this rule and feels that if the girlfriend were of Mexican descent, there wouldn't be a problem. Leorita recalled her husband's comments about bringing girlfriends over to their house:

> Aqui van a traer una muchacha cuando tenga sus dieciocho o diecinueve anos y que sea responsable y que tenga su trabajo y si piensa de casarse con ella?

> (Here you are going to bring a girl when she is 18 or 19 years old, is responsible, has a job and if he thinks about marrying her?)

> Probably not, because her parents would probably think the same way we do. Yes, it's hard for him, he can't deal with it and I don't blame him. But me, I would never dream of bringing a guy home, never.

Leorita has been involved with community activities and has served on various boards in the Hispanic community. She enjoys working with youth in different programs. Leorita sees herself as a role model but is cautious about taking on too much. She said that in the past anything that came up in the community, she was there to help. Now she realizes that others need to understand that they can help themselves too, "You guys have to fight for what you want. It will happen, if you fight and stay in, it will happen. Right now, we're working on getting some lighting for the neighborhood and maybe some speed bumps."

A striking example on a personal note for Leorita regarding being seen as a role model came with talking about her youngest child. Leorita said that she's always having meetings at her house and her child watches:

> When I was going to the meetings, most little girls play houses and dolls. My daughter is playing meetings. You know she sat all her little chairs around the table and all these stuffed animals. I asked her what she was doing and she said, " I'm having a meeting."

Another child asked her how to deal with prejudiced people. Leorita told him that you couldn't take them too seriously. She said that there will always be people like that and you can't let them set you back:

> There was a teacher who was prejudiced. She sat my son with other kids who got in trouble a lot; they happened to be minorities. Finally I went in one day and I told her you don't have to like everyone, but you're a teacher. I told her, you have all the minority kids sit at the same table, is there a reason? Why is it? That table is always causing problems. I'm not saying that my child is perfect, but when you sit in with other troubled kids, you're going to get big trouble. She was embarrassed, totally embarrassed. She apologized over and over again. Like I told the kids, nobody else is going to take care of it.

## "God is the Center"

Leorita said that being Catholic meant a lot to her. When she was young, her parents were Catholic in name only and she recalled walking to church to prepare for first Holy Communion with her siblings. Now she enjoys working with other people in the Catholic community. She helped a friend become Catholic by attending classes with her and being her sponsor, only to have the friend in the end not finish, but Leorita felt she learned a great deal:

> I got a lot out of it. I feel like I was the one that became Catholic. And so, after that, I've been very involved. I think God is the center of my life right now. I think once you're with God, you've got everything else made. It comes with family and it comes with everything else if

you put Him in front of everything else. My husband says that I don't worry, 'y tu ni te apuras tu no mas dormida', (and you don't even worry, you just sleep), I say, what is there to worry about? We only have what God wants us to have.

Leorita said that hearing the mariachi play captures certain feelings in Mexican people that can't be explained. The feeling is hard to express to someone who doesn't understand. She said that her older child was raised with less Spanish spoken in the home, but when the other children hear the mariachi, Leorita said it gets to the heart of them. When she spoke of her children, Leorita had special feelings for each of them. She said that if her oldest wanted to move out of the house, she would feel hurt:

> If my oldest child chose to live with us for the rest of his life, he'd be more than welcome. I can't understand the American way when they can't wait for their children to leave. To me, that is the most cold feeling coming from a mother. You know I hope they never get out of this house. If they're married and leaving, making their lives, going to school, that's different. But just to move out because they don't want to live here? I think that would be more of a hurt feeling for me, than it'd be a happy day. Here they look forward to that. And that's where I compare myself and say, " I don't understand you guys."

Leorita recalled an incident that occurred when they were visiting a state where there was a lot of Mexican people. She thought there wouldn't be any prejudice, because Mexicans were all over the place:

> We walked into a big restaurant, a pretty fancy place. It was an expensive place and we couldn't afford to stay there. We saw maybe a couple of Mexicans there, two or three families. We walked in and everybody notices you. And you know they were noticing you because you're Mexican. You know, I felt it. I know that was right. You just felt that's another thing I can't explain. I told my husband, never in my life were people so rude. I think it was because we were asking and we were Mexicans. I really feel that. Here I feel people are less rude. I thought it would be the other way around there. My husband said that maybe they're more on guard because there's so many of us there.

Leorita is so involved on so many levels, family, extended family, friends, community and the Catholic Church. She is balancing two cultures, American and Mexican. Although at times, she admitted that it is difficult because she understands both sides. Her family and the Latino community respect her for her commitment to fairness.

## VII: EL CUENTO DE EUFEMIA

## "Out of the Stream"

Eufemia is 37 years old. She has four brothers and sisters. She is an undergraduate student and also works as a staff secretary for a university. Eufemia's home was very comfortable. We sat in a room off the main living area where it was very quiet. Eufemia and her family were in the process of moving. In her other home, the woodwork resembled that of the other Latinas' homes, all natural woodwork and wood floors with an open, airy feeling with overstuffed chairs.

Eufemia began by telling me that she is Mexicano-Chicano. She was born in Texas. She still has many relatives there. She stated that her family was a migrant farm family:

> Our family would travel here to do their sugar beets, pick potatoes. They would also pick onions. They had picked cotton as well. And then they would come back, you know, at the end of the summer, or the migrant season, back to Texas. My father liked it in the Midwest and decided to settle out of the migrant stream when I was about four years old.

Eufemia's family were farm tenants and she said that working the fields meant, our pay was out there, food on the table for the summer. She remembered that her grandparents also came along and worked in the migrant stream:

> And so we all lived together in this little house when we first settled out. And I can remember still, living in a very small house, maybe it was two bedrooms, the living room and the stove was a wood- burning stove. You know where you had to have fire in it or wood in it to burn. I can remember having to heat the water so we could take baths in a round tin tub. It was like I remember and they were fond memories, it was a hard and difficult life, but there were still fond memories of that kind of life. Eventually my dad found a farmer who needed help. And we got to move into our own house. And, my grandparents still had the little house. We were still the field workers, I guess you could say until well into my high school years. By that time, my father was able to get his own farm. Be on his own, his own boss and farm. And we were able to have something to call our own.

## "We Have This Familial Support"

Eufemia recalled the farm crisis in the 1980s and said that her family lost the farm that her father loved so much, "You know, you have your whole life invested in growing things from the earth." Eufemia said eventually her dad took on a related trade in the farming industry and retired just recently. She said that her mother decided that she wanted to work outside the home after working in the fields with her father. Her mother decided that she wanted to work with the elderly and then proceeded to get more training to be a nurse's aide:

> She takes great pride in that. Even now, she's retired from the rest home, but she did work until a couple of years ago when she did retire. Right now she's on an on-call basis. She works part-time and she enjoys it. She just loves it.

Eufemia said that high school was a lot of fun for her, she made it fun. There weren't a lot of students perhaps forty in the graduating class. She attended a high school where there weren't many other Mexican students. She said that the Mexican students that were there usually stayed together. The teachers were fair but Eufemia stated that "some older ones had been there too long." Now, Eufemia's nieces and nephews attend schools where she went, and she hears them tell stories of the teachers that are there now:

> The drop out rate is real high. As they were going through grade school, the teachers there were very opinionated about the Mexican kids. You know, with the migrant students that settled out of the stream, some of them had difficulty with English. They were some-what racist and opinionated about how they can learn. Their teach-ing styles were left a lot to be desired. But then there were some schools, some teachers were really in there and really cared. So depending on whom you had for third grade or second grade made a difference.

Eufemia recalled an experience early in school, which affected her deeply. She stated that when she first started in her country school she was bilingual and perhaps spoke more Spanish than English. She said that she was chastised for talking Spanish and feels today that was one influence for her not being more fluent than she is right now. The feelings that she experienced then are still with her today.

Education was important to Eufemia's family but she said her parents didn't attend teacher's conferences or anything like that. When she told her father that she wanted to go away to college, a long way from home, he said:

> He told me, "well, you know, what you're doing is good." I was think-ing about going into business at that time, Business Administration. He told me to do my best and try my best there. I was going by myself to the university, no friends. He had bought me a car the year before to go to a community college close to home. And you know he told me, "make sure you call when you get there." But just to let me go like that, all by myself, was kind of hard for him.

After the first year of college, Eufemia thought this wasn't for her. She was too involved with the social part and not enough with the academics. Although there were mentors at this university urging her to finish and encouraging her to stay, she decided to go home and get married to her boyfriend. Eufemia returned home and worked for a couple of years saving for her wedding. She said she wanted to pay for all the expenses:

> I can remember telling Mom and Dad, we'll pay for the wedding and we don't expect you to pay for anything. And of course, you know, Dad with as proud as he is and you know mom too, we told Mom, we'll pay for all the food. We'll hire somebody to cook, because we want you and dad out there with us, just having a good time. Mom got so upset and she got mad. She said, "No, you will not. I want to cook. It's my obligation. That's what I want to do for your wedding." I couldn't talk her out of it. She felt it was part of what she was responsible for. So they went ahead and planned the menu. And she was there cooking with her commadres. Dad was there and said, "Well what all do we need?" And they started buying food right away, months before and freezing it, getting all this chicken and ground beef. It's like okay, you let them do that for you because you don't want to offend them and you don't want to hurt their feelings.

Eufemia said that living from paycheck- to- paycheck wasn't easy. She and her husband were finding it difficult to save in the jobs that they had. They both agreed that it was time to get back to school and get their degrees. Eufemia stated that it was difficult leaving home again because they had such a routine in seeing their parents so often. It has been five years since they left home and still Eufemia said it was very difficult to leave her family. Eufemia found a job with the university and it worked out perfectly, tuition was reduced for employees:

> My husband decided that school wasn't what he wanted and he went back to work. Being part of the university as an employee made it a lot easier for me. At this point, I 'm not ready to quit work and go to school full-time. Because, you, know financially we just couldn't cut it anyway. But you know I'm plugging away at it a semester at a time and a class or two at a time. You know I'll eventually get it. But he's real supportive in helping me go through school you know. He takes on the child-care. He'll cook you know, when it comes time to cook-ing. And he likes to clean. I mean, he doesn't like to clean, but he doesn't like a mess. And to me, a mess is a mess, you know, it can stay there, it doesn't bother me. But he's one of these cleanly people, you know. I have a real good support.

Eufemia reminisced about the role of her extended family. She said that extended family had been a part of her life throughout, starting with being a migrant worker. This past year two of her sisters completed their Associate's degrees. One sister wants to go on to get her bachelor's degree at the university where Eufemia works, she lives with Eufemia:

> So now, we do have that extended family again. And our families are living together, which has worked out real well because it's real difficult, they have three kids. It would be real difficult for them with just Marcos working, for her to go to school and manage the family and the home. It worked out real well. She goes to school full-time and I go to school part-time. But now we have this familial support too. We can count on the kids to clean and start supper. We can count on the guys to make supper every now and then and so we're back to an extended family again. My sister told me that once she gets her degree and finds a job and works full time, then I can quit my job and I can go to school full time. She said we can live with them and she can go to grad school and pay me back. I said, we'll just have to see how it goes along.

Eufemia is studying psychology now and expects to go to graduate school. She said that it's important for her nieces and nephews and her child to understand the importance of school. She said that her family is talking about UCLA and the University of Miami and she reinforces those dreams with them.

Eufemia's oldest brother stayed in his parents' hometown and helps the parents out a lot. Eufemia stated that her brother married out of the culture, but throughout the years, her sister-in-law has accepted some of the more traditional ways. Eufemia feels that her brother is a lot like her father, very traditional. Her sister-in-law makes tortillas and abides by the rules of her father in-law's home. Eufemia stated that her sister-in-law "hasn't taken away from his culture."

Eufemia talked about the traditional aspects of her family and what it was like in the past:

> I can remember as I was growing up that a lot of the things that happened in our home, to me, just didn't seem fair. You know, like at dinnertime, the men got to eat first. You know, my dad, my brother, and my uncles got to eat first. We'd have to warm up the tortillas or give them water, you know whatever they wanted to drink. We catered to their needs. And then after they were done eating, then it was the kids and the women. And as I got older, as I was growing up, I kept thinking, well, that's not fair. Why is it that they eat? Mom would say, well they're the ones that work out in the fields. And they're the ones that, you know, earn the money. And so they need to eat first to keep up their strength and so they can get some rest. She always had justification for our actions or what have you. We were migrant workers

and the money wasn't always there. Meat was limited they got to eat meat before we did.

Eufemia remembered that her father would go out with his friends on the weekends sometimes and come home and have her mother cook early in the morning for him. At these times, Eufemia said her dad would bring home beef jerky and things like that for the kids. This ritual continued until the kids were leaving the home and getting married. Eufemia stated that her mother always served her father, literally brought him his plate, but the kids would have to fend for themselves. She thought, "When I get married, it sure isn't going to be that way in my house. We're going to have equal say in everything." Eufemia said whenever they wanted to go out, her mom would always say, "Ask your dad." Many times he wouldn't let them go, but there was an alternative:

> So, it was always Dad's say, you know. We could count on mom to kind of talk him into it. If it was something we really, really wanted to do. So you know the authority laid a lot on dad. And what he said. And mom would be a real influential part of that yes or no. So she was always really the main focus. But she made us think that it was dad who had the final say. So I told myself and my husband always kids me about this, he says, you've made up your mind that you weren't going to be like your mom, you know. I'd be real strong-headed or pigheaded about something we're talking about and he always brings me back to that. I say, "Yes I know, but I am like my mom in a lot of ways. But, there were things that she did for dad that I would never do for you. So, don't expect me to."

## "Where We Feel Is Home"

Eufemia likes the traditions such as the quincinera. When a young girl reaches the age of fifteen, she celebrates the event with family and friends. She is also traditional in that she wants the family to stay together, as a unit if it can. Eufemia is also concerned about the high rate of alcoholism in the culture:

> You can never cure alcoholism. But if you can both work at the relationship and still not have alcohol as a problem, then the family should stay together as much as they can. Of course, there's a limit to everything. You don't stay in an abusive situation, if it's not going to work.

Eufemia talked about religion and how she doesn't attend church as often as she did back home. She feels that in the city where she lives now the diocese is too male-centered, she said, "It's not real you know, I don't see women up there reading Scripture and I don't see women giving the host or being laymen." At least her hometown church supported women in all parts of the celebration of the mass. She found it hypocritical to have strong beliefs about equality in God's eyes and then not see women involved other than the Altar Society.

Success to Eufemia meant being closer to completing her degree and having a job that she enjoyed. In a family sense, she wants to pay for her own house payment and not rent anymore, also having her husband be proud of what she does is important:

> I'd want him in a job that he's happy with. And my child hopefully would be doing well in school. Hopefully not in a gang and drug thing, keeping them straight and narrow path. That would be success to me. And then, being somewhere, where we feel is home.

Eufemia felt that there is a need in her hometown and knows that there is a lot to be done there too. She felt that the Mexican community could use her family's help. "You know that's what I've seen, doing naturally what needs to be done, so it would be helping my own people, I guess." Being a role model is important to Eufemia. She said that she enjoys watching the students come in as freshmen and then see them leave with a degree. She hopes that they see her as a role model, she said:

> I make every effort I can to meet those students that come from my part of the state. It's weird because some of them are children of my friends. It's just unreal, it's like, oh I remember when you were four years old, makes me feel old sometimes.

Eufemia added that she could hardly wait to read my dissertation because she felt that Latinas have something to contribute:

> Because I think we all come from different places. And we all have had different experiences. Mexicanos and Chicanos from other parts of the state and our experience are so totally different than, if you had grown up here in this part of the state. At least back home I see other Mexicanos. Here, I don't see them anywhere except when we go to Mexican dances. That's another thing I really miss when we moved here is, where is everybody? Where's my genta (people) you know? I think we need to go back home every now and then. You have to go home. You get kind of refocused about where we came from and what's important to us, because you get lost in that when you're not around family.

Eufemia said that her child would experience what it is like to be a migrant worker. She intends to send him back to his grandparents where he will get up early and work until sunset with only a thermos of water and tortillas with beans. She said that right now he has it easy, she said, "you will learn what it's like to be a beet-field worker." She said he hasn't gotten to that point yet, but he will. She will definitely make sure that he will. Eufemia shows others how the extended family plays an important role in the culture. Her roots are in migrant work and her discipline to persevere is attributed to this migrant life.

## VIII: EL CUENTO DE AURORA

## "I Want To Do It from My Heart"

Aurora's home is an older home with a huge fireplace in the living room. The room was light with white walls and an overstuffed sofa. The floors were natural oak and her home felt warm and inviting. I could imagine people just dropping over to talk. While I was visiting, Aurora was making homemade pasta and sauce, which she was very proud of. She is health conscious and has great concern about others' health too. Aurora is 23 years old and a graduate student. Aurora began her story by talking about education and what she desires to do:

> I was contemplating between law school and anthropology. Law school like the money and everything, you know, everyone's going to think you're successful because you're a lawyer, and especially coming from a Latino family. It's like, well you can do so much for Latinos, you can help them. I always found in my life people always telling me I have to help Latinos. I have to help this and that you know. I felt guilty for not wanting to do that. I mean, I do want to help people. But not just Latinos. I want to help everybody. And to me, Latino, that's my culture and I'm proud of it. That's where I came from. But I don't feel I should just section myself off from other people. That's why I want to go into anthropology, I want to do it from my heart.

Aurora spoke about how people today are materialistic. Achieving this goal of having a lot of things, they feel is success. Aurora felt that being happy inside is success, personal achievement instead of materialism is what she seeks. She said that she often remembers what Gandhi said, "Live simply, so that others may simply live." She is committed to helping the neediest people. The poorest are usually the people who are taken advantage of, so Aurora wants to help educate them:

> I want to help people. And I want to somehow try to alleviate the hunger problem, and at the same time, teach people to live with each other. I'm interested in getting into the Youth Peace Corps program. There's also one in Costa Rica. It's either that one or Alaska in the summer. You help the indigenous children in Costa Rica and you build schools and so forth. It's like volunteer work, you have to raise

$300 through fund-raisers for the trip and then you have to come
back and do 100 hours of social work in your community.

In her quest to help people, Aurora stated that she sometimes finds herself at
odds with developing relationships:

> I feel bad sometimes because I just kind of get so wrapped up with my
> needs and everything around me. I get too serious and I kind of push
> people out in a way. I almost feel like I'm scared to get involved with
> anybody because I don't want anybody to stop me. I don't want to
> feel, I just feel that I have a mission to do. And I have to get it done.
> And I know if I don't do this, I won't be happy, because I've denied
> my dream.

## "I Felt So Unfulfilled"

Aurora said that in high school she felt that people pushed her to be successful and go into law. She thought that if she had to have a job and be successful, yet help people, law was as good a profession as any other. She said
dating was not a problem because she never went out, until she went away
to college. A lot of people were asking her out and she felt like she was getting a lot of attention. She was totally sidetracked for awhile:

> Then after awhile it got really old, you know. I got too much atten-
> tion. I felt lost because no one liked me for who I was, for me. It was
> like, oh she's good looking and that was it, you know. I'd try to talk
> to them or get more serious, as a person, it's like they didn't want
> that. They just wanted a playmate or something. It really bothered
> me. I said I really don't like this, I don't like dressing up and being
> part of this. I don't really care about attention. I wanted somebody to
> care for me, for who I am. So it's kind of funny, because I always seem
> to go back to me.

Aurora felt that she came very close to becoming an alcoholic. She said
that was the way to deal with problems. Then one day she realized what she
was doing to herself and stopped. She was still very vulnerable when she met
and married her husband:

> I met my husband. He was somebody I'd known for a long time. I was
> hurting a lot and I was really sad. I really wanted someone to love me
> and I was going through a lot of pain. He kind of took advantage of
> that, and three months later I got married. I walked out of the judge's
> chambers and I said to myself, what did I do? This is the worst thing
> you could have ever done. But I felt that I had to marry him because
> I owed him, it's a long story. I think I held it against him and I hated
> him. I hated myself and the relationship kind of went down.

Aurora was very happy to receive a scholarship to another school. She felt returning to school was important:

> I was really happy to go back to school. Because, you know school has always been my drive, it's been my passion. I just love school. I love education. Back to my marriage, I tried really hard for my marriage despite how I felt. I felt when you get married it's for good. You get married and that's the way it is. I've always been strong about that because I come from a really strong family, as a matter of fact, my parents are still married. And they're Catholic. He (my husband) was from Mexico. And in Mexico they're traditional where the wife does everything. So I just started overworking myself. I was working from 30 to 50 hours a week. I was going school full-time. I was cleaning the house. I was doing the laundry, making him breakfast, fixing his lunch for him to take to work and coming home and making him dinner. And at the same time studying my homework in between. I was probably exhausted. I was very tired. All I wanted from him was maybe a little help and for him to take me out and do things. Most of the time he spent in front of the television or out with his friends and he'd totally ignore me. He never bought me Christmas gifts, birthday gifts, or anniversary gifts.

When Aurora asked her husband for a separation, she said, "he freaked out." He was concerned about not having his immigration papers in order and Aurora felt that she had been used in her marriage to him. Aurora was frightened of him because he threatened her and her family if she left him:

> It became a very violent marriage. For a whole year it was like the worst hell I went through. But ironically enough, the last semester before I left him, right before he got his green card, I had the best semester at my university.

Aurora felt that if she could make it through this marriage alive, she could make it through anything. She said she feels stronger now because of all her bad experiences and she's confident that she will make it. She felt that without the pain there would be no pleasure. Aurora knows that she's on the right path and even though at times it is still a struggle for her, she feels good.

## "I Did Instinctively"

Aurora told me that she wanted to do missionary work but her parents were very upset. She said all she ever wanted was to help people and that she didn't care about money or the prestige, her parents did. She looked around for another career and thought through advertising she'd be able to use her creative skills:

I love to draw. I love dancing. I love doing creative things. Somebody's telling me I'm a terrible writer, I write anyway because I love writing. It makes me feel good. I ended up getting into a big argument with the Business Administration lady and I said forget this, it's not worth my time. I don't feel like putting up with it for three or four years, whatever. So then there was communications and I thought I could be a newscaster or something. The more I did it, the more I realized it was like a totally shallow degree. There was no depth in it and it really didn't help anybody. Once I started going, it totally went against what I believed as a person. It was like, what am I going to do with this? It's like a totally selfish self centered degree. And you don't learn anything. I felt so unfulfilled.

Aurora had so many hours in this degree that she went ahead and completed it. She said that she learned a lot of negative things about advertising and communication, which is enlightening for her. She said, "It taught me to be more in tune with the things around me. It's the negative thing about it that taught me the positive."

Aurora had a very good friend who showed her how the simple things in life sometimes were the best things in life. She said she learned a lot from her friend but scared him when she started to give her things away:

> He made me look at my life and I just started going crazy. I just started throwing my things and started giving everything away. I probably freaked him out, because here I am totally wiggin' out because I don't know what to do because I was getting so frustrated. Oh my God, you know, I just want to get rid of everything, I just want to change and I didn't know how to stop. He gave me that push I needed because at the time I was so confused. I needed something. It's funny how life works. I feel like something's just guiding me through life because everything seems to always fall in the right place.

Aurora doesn't believe in God, but she does believe that "there's something out there, pushing me in the right direction." Aurora is intent about developing more of her creative skills and taking care of herself in a healthy way. She reads and writes poetry and recites her poetry before groups. She said her sister calls her a "granola head" but she doesn't care because it makes her happy. She runs in marathon races too and places highly for her age group. She said this about her activities:

> I guess that's where I spend most of my time, doing my hobbies. And I guess it's my way of shutting out people too. I mean, I always talk to people. I'm very congenial. I talk to everybody. But I never let anybody in. I don't let anybody get too close. Once they start getting too close, I run the other way. I guess, like maybe I said before, I'm scared

to get, let anybody know, because I have something to do and I have to get it done. And I don't want to get sidetracked, you know.

Aurora said that success is not money, position or power but finding self-fulfillment and happiness in yourself and what you do. She said that her perception of success wasn't always this way and she's learned what success means to her personally. Aurora remembered from the time that she was very young, fate has played a part in her life:

> I don't know, it just always seems ever since I was a little girl, in the second grade, we'd go to church and there was a song, "Let There Be Peace on Earth." That was my favorite song. Even when I was little, I was like three or something, my mom and dad told me I used to go to them and ask them for money. We were in Mexico and I'd go give it to the poor people who were begging. It was stuff I did instinctively without thinking about. No one taught me, I just kind of saw it and it didn't look right. I had something they didn't. I had to give it to them. I would pray at night, the first thing that I would pray for to God was let there be peace. I always felt that I was going to do something to help people. That's something I've always felt inside, deep inside me.

## "It's Like A Blessing in Disguise"

Aurora feels strongly that things fall into place for her even when the situation is frightening:

> After I left my husband, I felt like the worst thing in the world. I felt like dirt. I couldn't handle it. I was real upset. I was really sad. I thought I wanted to die and I've never been to that point. Literally, when I still believed in God, I went to church, it was like two, three in the morning or something. It was raining, I took off my shoes and just walked around in the rain. I walked into the church and laid on the floor in the church and I cried my heart out. I cried and I cried. I felt so lonely. And I just said, please take the pain away from me. I don't want to feel this pain anymore. I was so sad and lonely. I just thought I wanted to die. And so I went and bought these sleeping pills and stuff. I bought tons of them, it was funny because I was short on money and then this guy spotted my money for these sleeping pills. He didn't even know I was going to kill myself, he spotted me money. So I go home and start taking these pills. I had the Bible with me and I put pictures of my family, my nephews and nieces, everyone who meant something to me. I just started taking these pills and then I calmed down and I was in the middle of the pills and I realized, wait, what am I doing? I don't want to die. I go to this emotion I have for a split second. I'm like going crazy, oh no. I went and ran to the bathroom, I made myself throw up as much as I could. I was

so scared, because oh my God, I might die. I just finished taking these pills. So I called for help and told my sister's boyfriend that I had swallowed all these pills. I told him I want to go to the hospital to make sure I'm okay. I don't want to die. It felt good knowing I want to live. God I was extremely embarrassed, I didn't want anybody to know. But it taught me how much I valued life. I realized life is so special. It's like the best gift that you could have and throwing it away like that is just so foolish. And then it's funny how even in the worst times like that, how you just realize things. It just seems like all my life some kind of hope or something, somebody's out there. And after that happened, you know I started school. It just seemed to fall into place. It's like a blessing in disguise.

Aurora's parents have given her insight in a paradoxical sense she said. They always wanted her to become a successful and wealthy professional woman. They immigrated from Mexico with close to nothing and now they are successful business people. Aurora stated that, "And they have ironically taught me to be, externally, they taught me to be strong. They've shown me, if they believe in something enough, they can do it." The need to help people is so strong for Aurora that she feels that at times her family doesn't understand how great this need is:

It's hard. It tears me every time they put me down. It hurts because sometimes I walk alone. And no one's behind me. When I start doing things and they see the good things I'm trying to accomplish, I think they'll be very proud. They don't know it yet, but they will be. But I have to put my foot down. This sounds conceited, I don't want to sound conceited but I have a gift and a very special gift. I see myself talking to people and I feel like I touch people's lives. I know that everybody isn't able to do it. Someone has given me a special gift and I should use it to my best advantage. It's kind of like I don't understand it. It makes me feel good that I can make people feel good. It makes me happy. But again, I'm scared.

When Aurora had finished speaking she asked me why I felt that her life was important to write about. She believed that there was really nothing special about her. I was amazed that she felt this way after having endured several abuses in her young life. Aurora is a survivor.

## IX: EL CUENTO DE CHONITA

### "It Was The Most Enchanting Time Of My Life"

Chonita is 36 years old and a mother of two children. She works for a university as a counselor. Chonita and I sat at her kitchen table in the midst of the gray morning light from her windows. On a bureau in the corner sat several things, which were significant to Chonita; sage, stones, pictures of guardian angels and a candle of Our Lady of Guadalupe. She also showed me pictures of her family which showed me a great deal of how the family comes together. They gathered together in a park near a huge stone wall. Some family members wore no shoes and were very relaxed. It was a beautiful and stunning picture of a Latino family. I was grateful to Chonita for that image. Chonita began her story in a startling manner. When asked to describe events that were significant in her life, she replied, "My whole life has been significant." She said that her family came to the United States in an interesting way:

> On my father's side, they say that my great grandmother had to do a lot of different things to make money to get to the United States, that included some prostitution. She brought her two sons over. One son brought his wife over who is my grandmother. Now, I'm talking about my great grandmother because I knew her. So that was my great grandmother, and that's how on that side of the family we got to the United States. On my mother's side, my grandfather fell in love with my grandmother and stole her. He brought her to the United States and she didn't know where she was. On my mother's side they ended up having twelve children.

Chonita said that there was a neighborhood of many Mexican families in her city. She'll talk with students' parents now in her job and they remember what part of the city she's from and even know her family. She recalled with pride the only female Mexican softball team:

> We have pictures of it. We have pictures of my mom and that whole group. I guess they became the baseball champs one summer. They beat out every team. They were all a group of Mexican women. It was just real interesting.

Chonita's father was the second oldest son in the family. When his father passed away, Chonita said that the responsibility of the family fell on his shoulders because the oldest son was in a different state and had an established business made it difficult for him to leave:

> My grandfather was getting sick. I was probably three, it's real interesting because I remember this part, those last three years of my life, three, four, five almost into my sixth year, very well. Everybody moved in and little kids at that time are so self-absorbed anyway. To me it was the most enchanting time of my life. We moved in; and all of a sudden there were all these adults who just adored you. They were there for you, interacted with you on different levels and you knew what each of them expected from you. You knew the limitations and there was never any question as to what I was supposed to do. What I wasn't supposed to say and what I was supposed to say. It

just felt real normal and comfortable for me. And I think I remember those years of my life so much because there was such a cut-off later in my life. It was all a culture shock for me. My grandpa, when we moved in, I think I had just turned three, he was real sick, he was dying, related to diabetes. I remember that he got to the point where they were cutting off toes, those kinds of things. It was real common back then in the Mexican community. That goes back to saying how the health care was for our community, it wasn't very good. And a lot of it had to do with the fact that there wasn't much of a trust. There was a language barrier between the health community and Mexican community. I mean we're talking about first generation people coming over to this country and how we were seen as a labor, stoop labor. Back then as a kid none of that made any sense to me. But you know as you get older you start to read and you figure it out. You understand the concept of racism. You understand living in a bilingual world. In my home that's all they spoke was Spanish. My grandparents never spoke English to me. And they never, ever wanted us to speak English back to them. You know it was just a given. We were required to speak Spanish back out of respect. Well, my grandfather died. It was natural for us to move in, and my great grandmother and my grandmother were very close to my mother anyway. And it all just seemed to kind of fit.

Chonita's father passed away a couple of years later. Chonita felt like a lot of significant people were leaving her. Her father left a pension for her family and her grandfather left a life insurance policy, which paid off their house. Chonita was part of a three-generation household. She recalled that her mother didn't have any working skills and she didn't know how to drive, but she learned:

She had to hire someone to teach her how to drive. It all kind of changed but it stayed the same. The women in my life were still the strong forces. They were always the strong forces. I remember when people wanted to make decisions they'd always come to my grandmother and my great grandmother. And she was always the determinator. The person who would determine the final determination what people could and couldn't do . . . the approval person.

Chonita remembered that every Sunday after mass everyone would come over to her grandmothers and mother's house to eat. She said she didn't remember that much about the mass but she remembered everybody eating all day. She said her grandmothers and mother would go to early 7:30 A.M. mass and then come home to prepare everything, "You know, every Sunday it was just like a big family, festive thing." What Chonita remembers about going to mass with her grandmothers and mother helps her to cope now:

The thing I remember about church that was so interesting, is that when we'd go, there were times that I'd go to early mass with my grandmothers. They couldn't understand the priest but they'd sit there on their knees with the Rosary. They'd be saying the Rosary, you know, the whole time. I'd look at my grandmothers and think, how can you not respect women like that, you know, their beliefs and philosophy? You think about great leaders. They were my role models. When I think about strength, when I start to question myself or give up, I think about what they did to get to where they're at, that means nothing to anybody else but me, you know?

## "You're Mexican, Be Proud"

Chonita's grandmothers were concerned about the welfare of Chonita's mother and wanted her to remarry. Chonita's aunt would try to introduce her mother to eligible men. Chonita said when her grandmothers met her stepfather they felt he was the right one. Chonita said it was interesting because he wasn't from the Mexican culture but that didn't matter to her grandmothers. He was good to her and the children. He would be a good provider. Chonita said it was rare in those days to find someone for a mother of four children and to also be Mexican, her stepfather really loved her mother:

> He fell in love with my mom and so my mom married him. We moved to the other side of town, which was not really the other side of town, but it was way over there. For a kid it is. It's like Grandmother's way over there and we're way over here where there are no Mexicans. We were the only ones in the neighborhood. It was really different. We were all scared. You know it was interesting because as a kid, things change but you're not sure what really changed. What seemed to be a warm, relaxed environment where it was comfortable for everybody to discipline you or to take turns giving you a bath or take turns screaming at you, you know what I'm saying? It was an okay environment to an environment where this person comes in and they're disciplining you, but it's different. The discipline's different. The contact is different.

Chonita said that when her dad was still living and around her grandmothers, she just knew that she was to respect them and not talk back. She thought it could be attributed to being Catholic but she felt she always knew her place within the family. With her stepfather, she said she never quite knew what was expected of her and the communication was never there. She thought that it could have been the cultural differences:

> We were all thrown into a world where we just didn't understand. You know, all of a sudden we were sitting down to these big meals

where it was very white, middle class American meals. We were eating things that I had never eaten before, like steak. I was used to my grandmother's cooking, we'd go in and we'd sit down and there would always be tortillas, you know. Those things that were always comfortable for me, that were always there, there would be a combination of so many things that I knew what I could and couldn't eat. All of a sudden you had to have this on your plate and everybody sits there at the table and you're quiet, much different. But as time went by, the combination kind of came about. My stepfather had to learn that we were going to talk and we had to learn there were certain times that we couldn't talk. Whereas before when we were all together, we would just all talk. We would just all share.

Chonita said there were unsettling things that happened in her new home, such as her father walking around in his underwear sometimes. Chonita said that she was raised to be very private and dressing in front of someone was immodest. Her mother wasn't pleased by her husband's behavior but she taught the children to try to ignore it. Her mother didn't continue speaking Spanish to the children and Chonita said that it's rather difficult for her mother to talk about:

> Because all of us have had to go back and recapture who we are. You know, first we're Hispanics, then we're Mexicans, oh excuse me, then we're Mexican Americans and then we're Mexicans. Then we're Chicanos. Now we're Latinos. Each of us has had to scrape to get back to who we are and it's so funny. I can get really emotional about it, because I've seen what my sister has done. I've seen what my brothers have done. And I've seen what I have done. And each of us is struggling to get back to who we are. I know my mother did what she did because she wanted us to fit in. She wanted us to be successful, but I think she forgot that we had brown skin. Just because we might have come from one environment to another environment, that didn't change who we were. But my mom decided not to speak Spanish anymore in the house. She felt that it was disrespectful to my dad. That he wouldn't understand, so in that sense she was very much a Mexican wife, because to her everything is respectful, to the point that I felt like she lost her culture. My mother now says it's because we didn't want to learn Spanish, so she stopped speaking Spanish, but that's her way of justifying in her head. I went through a period where I was angry with mom for all of this. But then I kind of had to realize where she was and how she was caught when she made the decision that she made, so she had to adjust. We had to come along with her.

Chonita spoke of how her complexion confused people when she was little. She said everyone always asked her what she was. She said that she looks more Native American than Mexican and her mother is very fair in complexion while her father was very dark. She recalled telling others that she was Mexican:

> I remember as a kid, a Mexican-American. I'd say, a Mexican-American in an almost embarrassing way. Embarrassed because it was important for other people to know who I was and what I was, but I couldn't, I lost the language. When people talk to me in Spanish, I could understand more than I could speak.

Chonita explained that it was more of an emotional loss for her. Although she remembers in her grandmothers' home, if something happened, a candle was lit. There would be an altar in her grandmother's bedroom where the children would go to pray before bedtime. She felt that event was Mexican Catholic. Chonita sadly recalled that these events that were part of the home life kind of died away, but now her mother is bringing them back:

> There was always Mexican food around, for birthdays or for Christmas, we'd still do the traditional enchiladas and tamales. I guess the food part of it, Mom continued. I'm real grateful for that. With my kids, it's important that they know the language. I talk about our culture. I talk about the pride. My Mom never really talked about the pride. My grandmothers did, they'd say, you're Mexican, be proud, you come from a very rich culture and they'd say it in Spanish.

## "Being Ripped Between Two Cultures"

Chonita said that her husband acculturated into the Mexican culture a little bit too. At first he wasn't quite sure of all the extended family events. The hugging and kissing was also somewhat surprising for him:

> He didn't understand why people did that. And I'd say, that's part of our culture and it's okay. It does not mean anything other than that's how we care. We care to let relatives know we care. And that was one thing he had a problem with.

Chonita said when she met her husband she brought him home to her mother and family for them to give approval. She said she would never bring anyone home casually, but in the European culture she felt that people did this a lot. She said it really wasn't a big issue in that culture, but for us in the Mexican culture, she thought, "If I brought somebody home, it means that I'm serious about this relationship and so I wasn't going to get involved with anybody unless my family approved." Chonita commented that time orientation was also a difficult concept for her husband to process. She said that it wasn't a problem to arrive ten, fifteen minutes to a half an hour late anywhere. Whereas in her husband's family it was important to be a half an hour early or on time or it was seen as an insult. She believed that there are communication patterns that are related to cultural beliefs and the way you see things.

Chonita felt like a turning point in her life occurred at age 16. She was working in a factory and she got her hand caught in a machine:

> It was actually the beginning of me realizing that I could spend the rest of my life in factories, and doing things to my body, losing parts of my body, losing my mind, whatever. And going nowhere, doing nothing, which is what I was really doing. Or get my life together and go out there and do something for kids like me.

She finished her high school equivalency exam and started classes at a junior college. She said she was devastated when counselors at this college convinced her she would work better with preschool kids than in a human service program. Chonita was grateful that her father's Social Security benefits helped her go to college, she said, "I was able to live and go to college because of that. That's probably why I did so well in school because I held onto that. You know, my father died for me to go to college kind of thing." She just finished her associates degree when a position opened for an assistant supervisor over young children in a university setting. She said one of the benefits of working for a university was receiving reduced tuition:

> And one of the big benefits is taking classes for $3, a dollar a credit hour. You'd be a fool not to do that, right? I loved college. I love school. You know that was the thing for me when I went back to the junior college, l loved it. I ate it up. I remember going to school with all these young girls. They were looking at me like I was stupid because I really got into it.

## "You Just Don't Take Things For Granted"

Chonita recalled that one of her supervisors told her that she should go to college, a four-year college. She told Chonita that she didn't belong there working and she was above an Associates Degree. Chonita felt inspired by this woman and held onto that thought. She received a degree in Human Development and the Family but says that with more guidance from an advisor, she would have chosen psychology. She is satisfied with her career choices and said that she has worked in a variety of jobs. She felt that she owed a lot to her mother and grandmothers. Chonita thought that it is very important to know yourself and where you come from which related to her feelings regarding biracial kids:

> It's important that they know their cultural background. If they don't, they're going to get lost. They're not going to know who they

are, where they're going, or what they're doing. And they're going to be ashamed of either being white, or being of the other race, whether it's Mexican, Asian, African-American, Native-American. It's important from my own experiences. Being ripped between two cultures.

Chonita felt that much of her success comes from her grandmothers and mother. She said that success meant doing whatever you want to the fullest of your capabilities, "You just work hard, you do it, you don't do it halfway." She said that success for family meant different things. One sister likes to cook a lot, another feels success by being a good mother and another sister likes to redevelop houses. For Chonita, success is working with people:

> It's doing what you believe is important. What I do is when I work with people, and if I'm not doing what I'm supposed to do, then I shouldn't be doing it. Sometimes I work too hard, so other people might think that I'm a workaholic. I think that's just how I was raised. Getting up every morning and doing what I think is the right thing. Living the life that I want to live and making sure that my kids have that same belief system. That they're proud of who they are and go out into the world and do the things that they believe and take nothing for granted. You just don't take things for granted because we're all one step from being poor.

Chonita said that her success could be attributed to her family yet it is also because of her individual effort. She feels proud that she is the only one in her family to go to college. She felt proud about her accomplishment but was also aware of the "machismo" in her family. She went to her older sister for advice:

> It was just starting to take a toll on me and I went to see my older sister. I said, I don't ever want to try and prove that I'm better than the family because I'm not. I'm a family member. But I think when I come home and start talking about things, I make people feel uncomfortable. My sister said that there were a couple of things I needed to do. She said to just sit back and not always give out information that I've learned with some of my family members. She also said that she would talk to the family and tell them what I was doing was good. She told the family that I was the first and they needed to support me. I get choked up about it because I think if I hadn't gone to my sister, I wouldn't have graduated from college.

Chonita felt that going to her sister for help was significant. She didn't know if other Mexican families were matriarchal but it was for her family:

> There's always been a specific person that everybody went to. It's always been very matriarchal. It's always been a female. When my

son was born he had a lot of colds and stuff. My mom said it was because of the cats and I needed to get rid of the cats. All my sisters and aunts would come over and say it was the cats that bothered my son. It's because they were listening to my mom in terms of what her opinion was, whether she was right or wrong, that's kind of how the family went. So when my mom moved away, my oldest sister took over. It's never a spoken thing, but we all know who to go to when we're making a final decision.

Chonita said understanding the boundaries in her family is important. When she became a drug and alcohol counselor, her family felt uneasy. Chonita accepted that because some of her family needed to cope with their own situations regarding drug and alcohol issues. Once she understood what needed to be said, she felt better and so did her family, "I learned out of respect for my family, there are certain things that you cannot discuss sometimes. I didn't want that to die because of who I am."

## "You Turn To Your Spirituality"

Chonita thought the issue of discussing death in her family was a comfortable subject:

> When we're talking about death, it's not something that isn't talked about. I mean, it's not that we're afraid. With my ex-husband's family, they never talked about things like that. It seemed okay to talk about death and dying and where we go afterwards or what we believed about those things. Spirits coming back you know. My mom and grandmother always said that when you had the same dream over and over then somebody's going to die. With my mom it was tornadoes, with my grandmother it was bears.

Chonita said that there have been stories that have been passed down through the generations. She has listened to the same stories by other Latinos and wondered about these ghost stories, "The legends that have come down through our culture that are still with us today." She said that a professor told her once that these stories came from the Mexican culture and she didn't realize it. Chonita felt that because these Mexican stories passed down through the generations, death and dying discussions were common:

> I don't know if it's the same with other Latinos, but in our family, if someone comes back to visit you who has died, it's a message. You know they're trying to help you. When my mother first married my step-dad, my dad came back and visited her for quite awhile, to help her through it. My sister believes and I believe this too, in guardian angels. As a kid, I always believed that I had a guardian angel. When I was in a really bad relationship, my great grandmother would come

back. She was standing at the back screen door, I ran up because I was so excited to see her. All of sudden I realized she was dead and I got scared. She looked at me and got mad, and she started talking to me in Spanish. In the dream I understood. I woke up and I didn't understand anything, but I saw it as a warning to get out of this relationship. I don't know if it's just in our culture but we're more open to spirits.

Chonita had an altar displayed which featured candles with Our Lady of Guadalupe and sage. She said that her spirituality incorporates Native American tradition with some New Age philosophies. Her experiences with the Catholic religion have not been good. Chonita felt that she experiences being bicultural everyday, especially in the work environment:

I guess when I think about being bicultural, the pressing issue for me is what's going on with credentials. Because they have all these in academia anyway, all these credentials, therefore they assume, it's almost a rite of passage for the academia culture. And therefore, it's okay for them to be nasty, to be cryptic. And everybody else is supposed to be okay with that. Interaction with these Chairs of these departments has been a real eye opener for me. I feel like a third class citizen. Not only the first thing that they look at is that I have brown skin, but that I'm a female. It's just like coming into another culture and having to learn to be like them to survive otherwise you will be looked at as being, from their eyes, stupid, or unknowledgeable or passive. Where I come from is to respect people who were in positions that they knew about, no matter what it was. So you respect these people, but if they don't respect you for your specialty, your whole way of looking at them has to change or you won't survive. It's like this psychological process we have to go through to survive or else we're not going to make it. But then hold on to what we are too at the same time.

Other people of color supported Chonita and advised her to not to blame herself in these situations. She felt they were the people to whom she didn't have to explain how she was feeling, they just knew:

They listened. They supported me. That is where I am right now, personally, I don't want to acculturate into the white culture. I want to live a bicultural life. I want to be able to live in that world, because that's my bread and butter, but I also know I'm doing good things for my people. And so I have to figure them out. But I can't stop being who I am either. I have to be able to find the support systems, I think my spirituality is good there too. You turn to God. You turn to your guardian angels and you turn to the Virgin Mary, you turn to your spirituality, it's important.

Chonita spoke often of her children and how important it is to her that they understand and appreciate the Mexican culture. They are learning Spanish and Chonita said through some of her courses, her Spanish is improving as well. She talked about the invisibility of biracial children who are white and Mexican American:

> I think people have a tendency to think we don't exist, or that we're invisible as a culture. But we're a very strong culture. And they're wrong you know. We carry a lot of that with us and our kids will carry that with them. It's important to continue to give them what we are.

Chonita intends to see that her children and other young people that she works with are proud of their cultural heritage. She herself is learning something everyday about what it means to be Mexican- American.

## REFERENCES

Gusdorf, Georges. Conditions and Limits of Autobiography. In James Olney (Ed.), Autobiography: Essays Theoretical and Cultural (pp. 28–48). Princeton: Princeton University Press.

Maslow, A. (1968). Synergy in the Society and in the Individual. Journal of Individual Psychology, 20, 153–64.

Van Manen, M. (1990). Researching Lived Experience: Human Service for an Action Sensitive Pedagogy. New York: The State University of New York Press.

Watson, L.C., & Watson-Franke, M.B. (1985). Interpreting Life Histories. New Brunswick, NJ: Rutgers University Press.

# CHAPTER 5

# Summary of Findings and Themes

M ARSHALL AND ROSSMAN (1989) STATED THAT A LIFE HISTORY APPROACH IS USED across social science disciplines. Understanding such a text through the viewpoint of the informant is useful, firsthand information. Life history perspectives study the experiences of how the individual copes with life and society. Life histories elucidate problems and help capture the evolution of cultural patterns and how the patterns are linked to the life of an individual, their significance and the individual's reactions (Watson & Watson-Franke, 1985).

This chapter presents a summary of the findings as revealed through the life histories and as related to the grand tour and sub-questions. It also presents the themes, which emerged from the analysis. Finally, a conclusion discusses the implications for educators and helpers and for future research.

## THE GRAND TOUR QUESTION REVISITED

The author expected that the grand tour question, "How do Latinas perceive themselves through self-reflection, family, community, and work (work can be inside or outside the home) when they contemplate success?" would illuminate what forces guide Latinas to be who they are. Their historias as told by the author gives the reader special insights and privileges into these Latinas' lives. They viewed their lives through their families, communities and work. Their successes they attributed to happiness with self, with stimulating others, living healthy, being in relationships with others and also being honest with themselves to say they want more from their lives. They see themselves as successful women and attribute it to their parents and grandparents. They noted that their families sacrificed and worked hard to make a good life for them. All of the women felt a need to be helping someone else. They are all helping people, some are professionals and some are helping through a community effort. The Latino community and being a part of it was very important to these Latinas. Most of the women were educated in Catholic schools and had parents or significant others who encouraged them to proceed with their learning.

## The Sub Questions Revisited

The list of sub questions is important to review. The author desired to understand the following: (1) is self-concept a reflection of Latinas' family socialization patterns, (2) is this perception of self reflected through acculturation/biculturalism patterns, (3) does this perception of self reflect an affiliation with the community, in this case, the Latino community, (4) to what do these women attribute their success to: self empowerment, family, community, and (5) what is the holistic picture which emerges from the perception of these three systems coming together, if they do?

The following responses though brief, should reveal to the reader that these Latinas addressed the sub-questions throughout their life histories.

### FAMILY SOCIALIZATION

Family socialization patterns did manifest in the Latinas' self-concept. Ramona stated that a family value was "education, not only formal, but character development and cultural development." She thought what a struggle it might become to attempt to bridge two worlds together (her cultural world and the established academe) when she chose to return to graduate school. Gloria's family was "the priority" and everything else was secondary. She felt that being born in Mexico because her parents wanted all their children to be Mexican gave her a "sense of identity." She acknowledged that participating in cultural events and understanding the cultural values would establish, "a base for me to develop more in terms of opportunities."

Carolina and Aurora both had traditional families when it came to wanting their independence, Carolina recalled this event, ". . . my dad would get mad and I remember him saying something about always running around and not staying home . . . that's why I got my license so that I wouldn't have to be home all the time." Aurora said that her family's progress in this country after immigrating from Mexico helped her understand her goals, ". . . they have ironically taught me to be . . . they taught me to be strong." Their wishes for her career and Aurora's dreams clashed as she began to demonstrate more personal independence.

Eufemia's family believed in helping each other out, in part this may be attributed to her family's migrant work which brought them closer together, she said, ". . . we all lived together in this little house . . . we were still field workers until well into my high school years." Eufemia's sister and her family are living with Eufemia while she (the sister) finishes her college degree, she stated, "we have this familial support and so we're back to the extended family again." The author feels fairly confident that family socialization patterns with a unique Latino stamp upon it, did impress these women to further their ambitions, albeit away from the family's norms in some cases.

## ACCULTURATION/BICULTURALISM

Chonita vividly stated what she perceived as an important difference between the Mexican culture and what she called "the dominant culture." She stated this about respect, ". . . when I think about being bicultural, the pressing issue for me is what's going on with credentials . . . it's okay for them to be nasty, to be cryptic . . . where I come from is to respect people but if they don't respect you, your whole way of looking at them has to change or you won't survive. It's like this psychological process we have to go through to survive. . . ."

Leorita painfully stated, "I really feel like I don't have a culture. I feel like I'm caught in the middle . . . I don't agree with everything in the white culture, that's just not me. But yet I can't deal with just the plain Mexican culture either . . . you know sometimes it's real hard."

Mary started to find out more about the Mexican culture while attending college and reading her deceased brother's writing about the family, she said, "I wasn't really in touch with my heritage or my identity as a Mexicana . . . I was very in touch with my American culture . . . I didn't feel a loss or not accepted by the American culture, maybe I was naive . . . it just dawned on me, I am 100% Mexican, then I felt this enormous loss . . . it was a total crisis for me." These statements painfully mark what the processes of acculturation and biculturalism may feel like to these Latinas. Imagine straddling cultures and wishing desperately to know which one will help you fit in the best. Psychologically we all attempt to produce environments and situational activities which allow us to feel less cognitive dissonance. When some of these Latinas struggle intensely with qualifiers such as "respect" and "humility", one can easily understand the stress which accompanies the question: "Do I trust my instincts or do I take risks that I won't be hurt?" Recalling Ramona's feelings regarding "universality" and being indigenous, speaks to us of the strengths of being Latina. Incorporating other cultures, the blending and beliefs assist Latinas in their journey toward self appreciation and identification.

## COMMUNITY

Did Latinas' perception of self intersect with involvement in the Latino community? Unequivocally these Latinas demonstrated a commitment to the Latino community. Carolina said that working with other Latinos helped her to appreciate the "family-like atmosphere" that was shared, "Because we were all Latinos, I never had that before. Just the way we were able to relate to each other was so much fun . . . you can have that with other people of color to an extent, but it's so different with your own." Carolina felt strongly that "contributing to the community was very important." Mary's commitment to the community was being asked to speak frequently to Latinas who were recovering women (substance and drug abuse). She said that she didn't quite understand it, but there was a special bond that connected all these Latinas together, she said, "It's really eerie because these women are from different parts of the state, of the country." Leorita has served on community boards in her city and has been involved with Hispanic organizations. She said she sees herself as a role model for the community, but wants the Latino community to stand up for their rights too, "You guys have to fight for what you want."

Gutierrez (1990) suggests modalities that utilize women of color uniting with other women in small groups, are the ideal intervention strategy. Gutierrez states that the small group, ". . . can be the perfect environment for raising consciousness, engaging in mutual aid, developing skills and solving problems can assist the individual in achieving personal effectiveness while influencing others" (p. 151). Apparently these Latinas in one situation or another have followed Gutierrez' advice and have practiced small group work principles. They have been involved with helping their families, communities, churches, and many other organizations.

The author's interpretation of these Latinas' commitment to community affirms what was found in their stories. Each Latina felt compassion toward their community. They see the world through their cultural lens, and it doesn't seem likely that they will acculturate so deeply to the non-Latino American culture that they will lose their sense of Latina identity. They are symbolically attached to giving. Their families of origin helped create this acknowledgment of giving back to others.

## ATTRIBUTIONS OF SUCCESS

The final sub questions were interrelated. The questions posed regarded what these Latinas attributed their success to (self-empowerment, family, and community) and what is the holistic picture that emerges from this perception? These Latinas attributed their success to pride in themselves, their families, and the Latino culture. The holistic approach to success was developed from their insights about these three systems. Ramona spoke seriously about the connections of "indigenous peoples" from the past and Latinos now whose attitudes about life intersect in profound ways. Carmen attributed her self-empowerment to her recovery program, her strength in overcoming the negative voices of the past and finding out more about the culture. A unique event occurred to Carmen in the summer of 1993. She traveled with another Latina to a conference in the South. There was a change of flights in San Antonio. Her companion exclaimed when they boarded off the plane, "Look at the beautiful brown faces!" Carmen realized that in the past being brown didn't feel beautiful. Now she feels an appreciation for who she is. Gloria sees the relationships that she has with her family and the community as strengthening "the cycle." She said that in the young girls she works with, "I see myself." Someday she sees those young people taking over what she has started and she'll be in another position to help more people. Carolina sees her empowerment in a bicultural attitude when she says, "I can show other Latinos that they can be independent . . . I think that they can maintain the culture and still take things from the dominant society too." Carolina also identified herself as a Chicana, she called it, "an ethnic consciousness term, which means that she's proud to be of Mexican descent and committed to her heritage." These words evoke a very powerful self-concept.

The author perceives that these sub-questions were answered thoughtfully by the Latinas. The intersection of empowerment, family and community enhanced their perceptions of cultural dimensions. Some of the women felt that they were firmly grounded in their cultural orientation, and others were only beginning to recognize how Latino culture (specifically Mexican American) affected their lives. When we believe in our ability to shape and form our lives, there is nothing more powerful. The term empowerment is a term that is often used in the social sciences. The power of the word evokes strong feelings of capability and efficacy. To visualize empowerment and see the benefits of the attributes is indeed quite empowering. These Latinas are living their empowerment, and they are role models for others to emulate and follow.

## THEMES

"The systems perspective examines the interrelationships between smaller units of analysis, operate within an enveloping environment and are affected by the environment" (DiNitto & McNeece, 1990, p. 51). The concept of utilizing a systems perspective by acknowledging how Latinas' lives evolve and revolve is appropriate to demonstrate through life histories. Understanding the women's historias came through hearing, reading and re-reading their stories. The process of defining and identifying these central concepts and themes was investigative and comparative. Attending to the historias of these Latinas with a careful ear assisted the author in the development of the analysis utilizing a graphic, circular design, which corroborated the historias. The process included a systematic approach of coding and re-coding the Latinas' texts, and analyzing the terms and concrete statements. Greater attention was given to the intuitive nature of this process as I recalled each of their voices and the passionate delivery that each gave when they discussed a subject about which they felt deep emotion. I agonized over the delivery of their stories to the printed word, thus, I checked with some of the women as I developed their stories and the analysis. This process is referred to as a member check process (Merriam, 1991). I felt relieved when they affirmed that I captured their feelings.

I contemplated visually how I would like to see the women's historias as represented to the reader. I envisioned a central theme and projections of that main theme into other circular patterns (see Figure 1). The graphic analysis that is represented is true to that vision. The smaller circles signify what thematic representations occurred throughout the life histories of these women. The text included in the circle represents the contextual nature and the womens' interpretations of those events. According to Van Manen (1990) phenomenological research is the study of "essences" (p. 10). Phenomenological methodology attempts to discover the meaning of lived experience. The central circle is the core of the women's nature regarding how they view success, what I see as the "essence" of the Latinas. The central essence is the bond, which holds all the other systems together as one sees the themes from a larger perspective. I mentioned to one Latina who was interviewed that I saw her "essence" (the central circle) as the sun and the revolving life events/smaller circles as planets, "a Latina solar system." She enjoyed that visual image and stated that the vision was really powerful.

**Figure 1: Illustration of Themes**

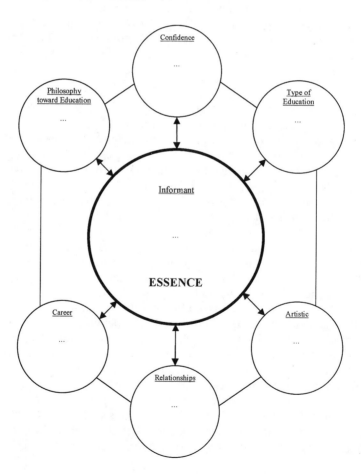

I felt that utilizing a systems approach in identifying central themes and events would clarify for the reader what experiences were important to these Latinas. A strength of life history methodology is that since it pictures the total course of a person's life, the reader enters into the same experiences. Life history methodology emphasizes the value of a person's own story and provides pieces for a mosaic or total picture of a concept. Interconnections of apparently unconnected phenomena can be seen. Mandelbaum (1973) suggested three alternatives to chronological order as a way to organize and present data: (1) the dimensions or aspects of a person's life, (2) the principal turnings and the life conditions between turnings, and (3) the person's characteristic means of adaptation. Mandelbaum's suggestions assisted me in organizing the process and approach to fully understand and analyze the Latinas' historias.

My intentions have been to create a visual representation of thematic patterns that emerge from these Latinas' "historias" (life stories). Life history methodology invites the reader to enter a relationship with each informant and live vicariously through each life. Each design exposes some similarities and differences amongst the women, and when seen as a group, certain dimensions of "Latina-hood" can be distinguished. Attention to the cultural, social interactions, family, where their confidence generates from, and what success means to them in a personal manner, may assist educators, social scientists and others in gaining an introspective perspective about Latinas.

The following information provides the reader with the dominant themes: relationships, philosophy toward education/type of education/careers, confidence and artistic natures. The interconnections of those themes within a larger system referred to as essence is examined. Each of the Latina women is represented in the Figures which follow. (See Figures 2–10)

## RELATIONSHIPS

### Acculturation and Biculturalism

These Latinas shared similar histories. As I was writing their stories, I could hear the voices from their past, great-grandmothers, grandmothers, mothers, and fathers all supporting them to speak their voices. They have all lived in the United States most of their lives. Undoubtedly, this has affected their levels of acculturation. Mary had strong feelings about living in two cultures, she said, ". . . being American, I'm real in touch with my American culture and am comfortable with our traditions and the so-called feminist movement, just knowing on the inside who I am and what I am and that no matter where I go in the world, it really doesn't matter because I'm confident within myself . . . I feel like I'm kind of on the outside looking for my culture, trying to bring it on the inside." Leorita felt that understanding and living in two cultures brought out these feelings, "I really feel like I don't have a culture...I feel like I'm caught in the middle."

To illustrate how acculturation affected Mexican-American families, Rueschenberg and Buriel (1989) conducted a study to investigate the relationship of acculturation to family functioning. They were interested in family interactions within the family context and family interactions outside the family. The findings suggested that external family variables such as independence and achievement orientation and acculturation were, "all in a positive direction, that is increasing levels of acculturation were associated with higher scores on the external variables" (p. 240). The results for the internal family variables such as cohesion and expressiveness indicated that," the basic family system remains relatively unchanged during the acculturation process" (p. 241). The authors agreed that a bicultural approach to understanding Mexican-American families is appropriate and that future study on the Mexican-American family should show more attention to those areas in which the family changes with levels of acculturation.

Bicultural orientation proved shocking for Chonita when her mother first married her stepfather. She recalled being pulled away from the only family she had ever known (her great-grandmother and grandmother) into this, "we were all thrown into a world where we just didn't understand . . . all of a sudden we were sitting down to these big meals where it was very white, middle class American . . . much different." Gloria felt that being in "two worlds" was a constant struggle within herself and said, "sometimes only people who live it, understand it." This is what Carolina has referred to as "cultural schizophrenia," feeling marginal. Regarding mental health issues, Latina women are at a greater risk because of the depressed socioeconomic conditions as well as role conflicts experienced as a result of migration and acculturation (del Portillo, 1988, p. 235).

## Feelings of Loss, Anger, Sadness

Blea (1992) stated that "being able to function in at least two languages and two cultures has not to date been a valued characteristic in this country" (p. 121). Language was a pivotal issue in the women's historias. The womens' parents spoke Spanish. Some women were bilingual and others were only English speaking, but made it clear that they wanted to learn and speak Spanish. Mary felt a sense of loss and also anger because her parents "wanted to give her an edge" by not speaking Spanish when she was young, she said, "I just want to say to mom and dad, why didn't you speak Spanish when I was little . . . I think it's interesting how generations afterward still feel the effects of that in one way or another.

Leorita felt that seeing Mexican people who don't speak Spanish is discouraging, "That's just a sad feeling to me, not being able to speak Spanish." There was a sense of regret on both sides of the issue. Bilingual speakers felt that other non-bilingual speakers have "chosen not to speak Spanish." In the reality of this issue, it is not the desire *not* to learn, rather while the women were children, Spanish wasn't spoken for a variety of reasons, such as dis-

**Figure 2: Ramona**

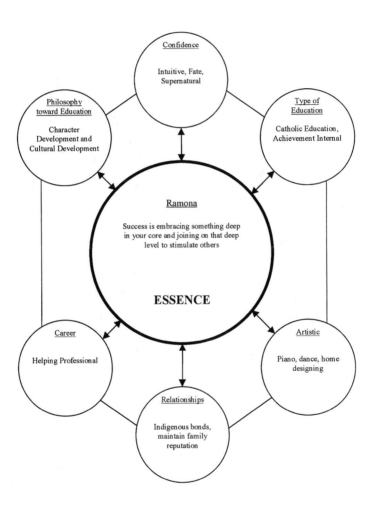

**Figure 3: Carmen**

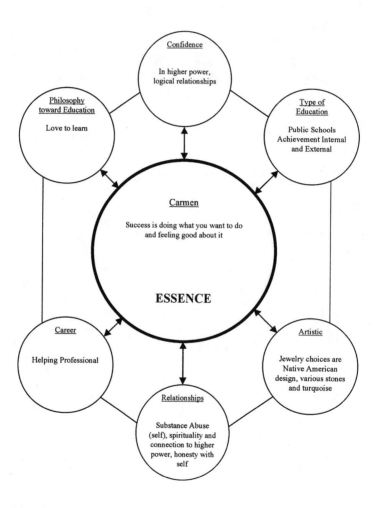

**Figure 4: Gloria**

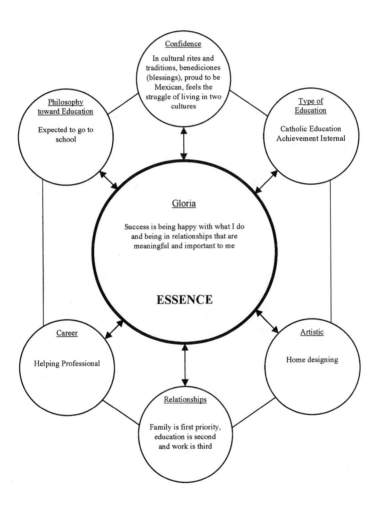

**Figure 5: Carolina**

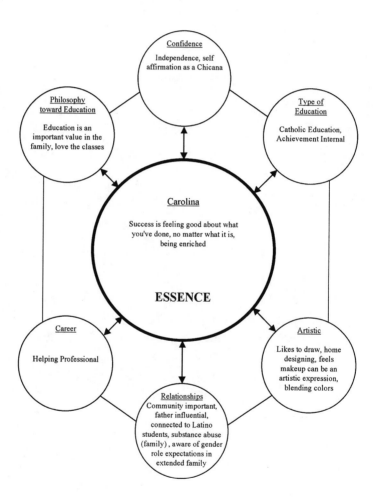

**Figure 6: Mary**

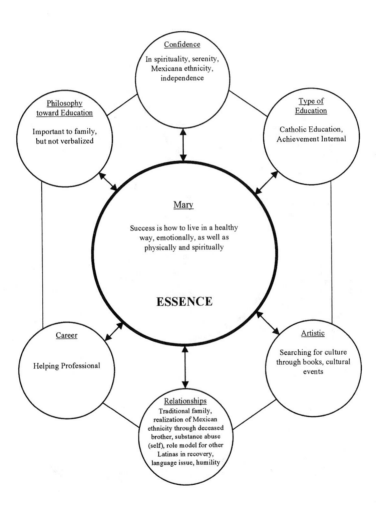

**Figure 7: Leorita**

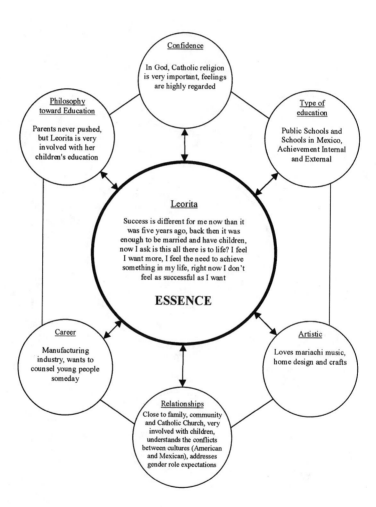

**Figure 8: Eufemia**

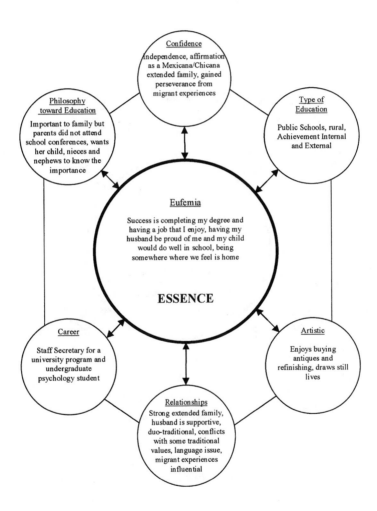

**Figure 9: Aurora**

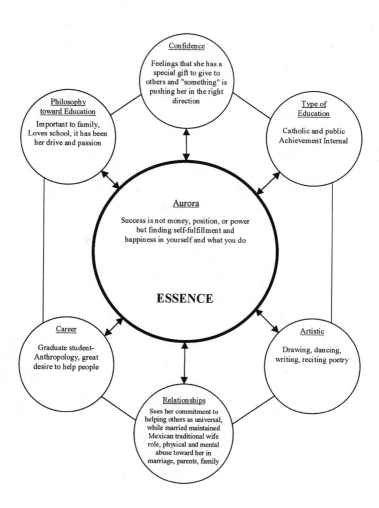

**Figure 10: Chonita**

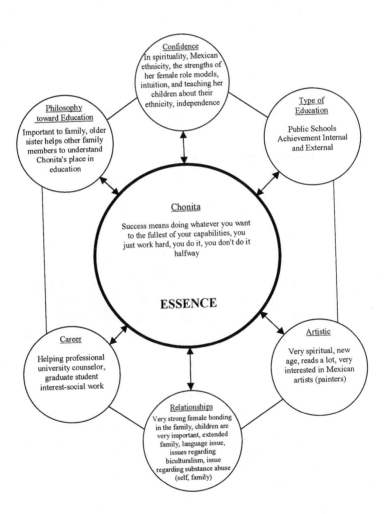

crimination. Chonita said that her mother wanted her children to be successful, so she stopped speaking Spanish.

Chonita also felt that her mother didn't want to show "disrespect" toward her stepfather because he was not bilingual. She felt a lot of anger toward her mother because of this, "I went through a period where I was angry at mom for all of this . . . but then I had to realize where she was, and she was caught." This feeling of being "caught" between two cultures was a predominant theme in most of the Latinas' historias. "Caught" is an interesting word as it was used to describe what it felt like to be between cultures. Aurora stated that her parents wanted her to be an attorney to help Latinos. She wanted to help the community and others too. Chonita felt that it was important to know where you came from which impressed upon her the need to educate biracial children, she said, "It's important that they know their cultural background, because if they don't, they're going to get lost . . . being ripped between two cultures."

## Discrimination and Self-Esteem

Blea (1990) stated that racism is multifaceted. The women had incidents with racism and discrimination that affected their families of origin or themselves. Some women commented that the complexion of their skin brought out these issues more clearly. Chonita said that when she was little she remembered being asked, "What are you?" She recalled feeling embarrassed about saying that she was Mexican American. She also said that her mother did what she thought was good for the children, Chonita said, ". . . she wanted us to fit in, she wanted us to be successful but I think she forgot that we had brown skin and just because we changed environments didn't change who we were." Carolina referred to an event that occurred while she was guest speaking about Latino cultures, a Mexicana teacher from Mexico was very angry about her presentation. Carolina stated, "I recall that she was light skinned with dark hair and I didn't know that she was Mexican. She just raised her hand and said, 'where do you get all your information, because none of that's right.' My heart was just pounding." Situations such as these caused great internal conflict among some of the women. Mary stated that complexion was a sensitive issue, she said, "I think it was easier for me to be a part of the American culture and feel more accepted because I am lighter skinned . . . that brings up a lot of feelings within myself too." Carmen eloquently and sadly recalled how she interpreted her stepfather's comments about Mexicans, she said, ". . . my best bet, the only way I was going to make it in this world was to tell people that I was not Mexican. . . . I was criticized real harshly when I got dark from being in the sun." On one hand, people were interested about their ethnic background out of non-judgmental curiosity, while on the other hand, people from the same ethnic background felt it was a duty to correct what they saw as a misinterpretation in front of others.

This points out another concept which women were aware of, the feeling of "tooting your own horn." The author's interest about this term was stated differently, it was called "humilidad" (humility). In Carolina's particular incident, she was surprised that this woman would openly embarrass her in front of this class of educators, she felt the woman was without humility or ready to toot her own horn. Mary stated that an opportunity for a new job was coming up and she felt uncomfortable because it meant, "tooting your own horn." She said, "I guess it has always been taught to me that you stay humble."

Turning points or significant life events have affected these Latinas perception of themselves. A majority of them have either had problems with substance abuse personally or their family members have had problems. They have come from traditional Mexican families and understand the strains of acculturation and biculturalism as first, second and third generation Latinas.

## EDUCATION/ PHILOSOPHY TOWARD EDUCATION/CAREER

### Expectations, Goals, Meanings and Connections

It was fascinating to note that the Latinas professed strong needs to do well in their careers and weave the culture into their success. Vasquez (1982) found that academically successful Chicanas felt identification with their cultural background. Buriel (1982) explained that acculturating Mexican-Americans who maintained a connection with the traditional culture were better able to defer negative images of Mexican Americans in American society. In Chonita's historia, this desire was clear when she discussed working in mainstream society while feeling this, "Where I come from you respect people who were in positions that they knew about, no matter what it was. So you respect these people but if they don't respect you for your specialty, your whole way of looking at them has to change, or you won't survive. It's like this psychological process we have to go through to survive or else we're not going to make it. But then hold on to what we are too at the same time."

Most of the parents encouraged education for their children and some were not quite sure of the process. Leorita stated that, "my parents never pushed when it came to education." Gloria said that, "education was an expectation." Ramona stated that, "a college education was a family value" and Carmen felt that she "didn't fulfill her potential as a child in her early education" but she is "in love with learning." Now in their lives, the women understand from an adult perspective the importance of education and those with children are securing that position as they become parents. Senour (1977) stated that ". . . the Chicana is a product of two cultures; traditional Mexican American culture, which she may experience at home although frequently in diluted form, and dominant American culture which she experiences almost everywhere else, especially at school" (p. 331). Several studies on Chicana achievement point out that Chicanas' mothers can make an impression on their daughters' aspirations. The levels of education received by the mothers influence their daughters' achievements. Gandara (1982) reported several factors which contributed to Chicanas' high achievement which included role-modeling by their mothers. Latinas who were interviewed for this study had mothers who were not college-educated, but they believed in their daughters and encouraged them in many ways. Chonita recalled how her grandmothers were the people that other family members looked to for advice. Other people influenced these Latinas including fathers and grandfathers.

Ramirez and Price-Williams (1974) conducted an investigation examining white, Black, and Mexican American fourth grade children regarding achievement motivation and family identification. Their arguments involved three factors: (1) a definition of achievement motivation is rooted in a western view of psycho-dynamics, defining human behavior as individually motivated, (2) contextual conditions are more important in the expression of achievement motivation, and (3) the particular form in which achievement is expressed is determined by the definition that the culture assigns it. Ramirez and Price-Williams (1974) concluded that blacks and Mexican Americans expressed achievement motivation in the form of family achievement. Gloria affirmed this conclusion clearly when she said, "There really wasn't a sense of identity (at the school she attended), I felt like I didn't know who I was even though my family was traditional . . . at the Center, I found myself, I see with other young women the effect that I can have on their lives . . . they're like an extension of my family." Gloria as a representative of the culture assigns importance to receiving an education to the young women that she works with, they in turn, value what Gloria says and continues to encourage others. Gloria stated that it was a cycle that will continue. In terms of academic achievement, all the women expressed an interest in higher education. Some are currently in their undergraduate and graduate programs.

A few women in this study commented about how the Latino community was important to them. Often the community is referred to as "la familia" (the family). Carolina felt very strongly that her academic success would help the community, "Something that's important to me is to contribute to the community. So now the skills that I'm learning can be used in the community." The Latinas' views of their families of origin often intersected especially when they spoke of hardships on the family because of economic conditions and the desires their families had toward their childrens' academic success. Their parents were mostly immigrants and all were working class. Gloria stated that her grandparents were so poor but they were happy. She said this about her parents who left Mexico and their families, "They sacrificed their relationships with their parents . . . knowing that Mom and Dad came to this country to give us a better life." Two of the Latinas had parents who were migrant workers. They had special feelings regarding this, Eufemia stated, ". . . our pay was out there, food on the table for the summer. We all lived together in this little house . . . it was a difficult life but there were still fond memories of that kind of life."

Cummins (1986) proposed a variety of factors including inter-group power relationships that contributed to the lack of educational success of Latinos. He studied Finnish students' academic achievement in Sweden where they had relatively poor academic performances and they are also considered a low status group. In Australia they are considered a high status group and their academic performance was more successful. Cummins stated that since a change of status is not foreseeable at this time for Latinos in the United States, he suggested several propositions to empower Latino students: (1) incorporate the language and culture of the minority group into school programs, (2) advocate that the ethnic community of the student participate in their education, (3) implement methods to increase motivation by advocating that students use their native language to achieve greater knowledge, and (4) rely on paraprofessionals in the ethnic community regarding assessment of issues instead of standardized tests to localize problems in the student. Cummins' suggestions are well received already by some of the Latinas who work in programs that advocate exactly what Cummins' proposed. These particular Latinas are role models in their programs and are proud to work with Latino students. Carolina remembered when she started working with Latino students, ". . . I was a little intimidated at first, but once I got to know them, I liked them a lot. I always tell this to people, that I never really felt my culture. . . . I didn't think my family was traditional until I started working with the girls . . . I started feeling like I could relate more to somebody . . . I was connected to somebody." Eufemia and Chonita have the opportunity to assist college-age students. Some of them are children of their friends, Eufemia said, "It's weird sometimes . . . it's unreal, I remember when you were four years old, makes me feel old sometimes."

It was quite interesting that all of the Latinas except one would be considered helping professionals. Perhaps this was due to the author's disposition as helping professional and other referral sources who assisted in identifying potential informants. The sole Latina who was not a helping professional stated that she wanted to return to school and be a counselor for the youth. The women found helping others very rewarding. Ramona stated this about helping others, "I now realize that I never abandoned the call to understanding the nature of the human psyche . . . an expression of my soul." Aurora felt that her family someday would realize the intense desire that she has to help people, she said, "This sounds conceited, I don't want to sound conceited but I have a gift . . . a special gift. I see myself talking to people and I feel like I touch people's lives." Combined with their intense regard toward higher education, these Latinas' career choices pointing to the helping professions could certainly add new dimensions to this field.

Garcia (1990) stated that attempts have been made to bring Chicanas back into history. Garcia notes that this omission of learning about Chicana leaders has created an imbalance, which has contributed to the negative stereotypes regarding Chicanas (p. 20). Many of the Latinas felt that they were role models in their families and communities. Although some of the women felt somewhat surprised when the author asked if they considered themselves as role models. Mary felt very surprised, "Oh wow! I guess I never really thought that I was a role model until last year . . . by sharing my experience, strength, and hope (regarding recovery from substance abuse), then yeah, I am a role model." Carmen viewed being a role model in this way, "I really have a desire to work with those people (prisoners) because they are like me . . . I also felt that I could never be successful . . . I am such a different person today than what I used to be and it feels good."

## ARTISTIC

The author was interested in how the Latinas expressed themselves artistically and if that was an important part of their lives. The author noted that the Latinas' homes mostly reflected a traditional old home structure with the natural woodwork, wood floors and comfortable furniture. This choice of home style and decor was fascinating to note while talking with the women. Their artistic natures ranged from home designing, drawing, reciting and writing poetry, reading about Mexican culture and artists, dancing, listening and playing with the mariachi. The author was intrigued by how many similarities there were in reference to artistic natures.

## CONFIDENCE

The thematic representation of how the Latinas gain their confidence was important to understand. God, the Catholic religion, the supernatural, in cultural rituals and blessings (bendiciones), Mexican ethnicity, independence, fate, and intuition contributed to these Latinas' strengths. Ramona felt that, "fate can be either conscious or unconscious effort and having a vision . . . that's what fate is, it's magnetizing things to you." Ramona also said that her mother used "mother radar," an intuitive approach. Gloria's interactions with her husband's grandfather in Mexico gave her inspiration when he blessed them both, "There was something about his knowledge, about respecting him . . . the bendicion is something that I'll always remember . . . everyone knelt down when he gave it." Leorita is a strong Catholic and said that her faith means a great deal to her, "I think once you're with God, you've got everything else." Leorita also said that hearing the mariachi play evoked special feelings within her and her children, . . . when the children hear the mariachi, it gets to the heart of them, the mariachi captures certain feelings in Mexican people that can't be explained." These significant statements fascinated the author. The acceptance upon the "unexplainable and reliance on intuition" may contribute to how these Latinas make their choices and live their lives. Chonita recalled a dream that she had about her great-grandmother, "She was standing at the screen door . . . she started talking to me in Spanish, in the dream, I understood. I don't know if it's just in our culture but we're more open to spirits."

Confidence is also a measure of one's maturity. In these women's stories, each had a "baptismal fire" in their lives. They felt assured that they could meet each challenge with success due to their family's support, and their unique abilities to assess situations.

## CONCLUSIONS AND IMPLICATIONS

### Future Research Initiatives

A stranger asked the author about this research she said, "What kinds of things did you find?" The process of writing these Latinas' historias and searching for the truths in their stories was an exciting and exhausting task. As the author was attempting to understand the "bigger picture" she felt caught up in the voices and it was difficult to "hear" the "cuentos." So when this stranger asked this most simple question, the author immediately realized that these life events as told in the women's individual voices could be heard through group voices too. I could close my eyes and listen and hear similar stories. The women, for the most part (majority) do not know each other.

### Suggestions for Educators, Helping Professionals, and Others

This would be useful information for future research regarding attitude toward language acquisition, language maintenance, bilingual education programs, and acculturation patterns, which create stress for non-bilingual Latinos. These women were acculturated and bicultural. It would be worthy to note that these second and third generation Latinas felt loyalty to the Mexican culture and were not Spanish speaking. Language is very important because it assists in the transmission of culture but these Latinas transmit culture utilizing other means too, such as working in the Latino community, taking pride in cultural events, speaking about the culture, and being a role model for other Latinos.

Helping professionals and educators should note that acculturation processes for first, second, and third generation Latinas is an important issue. The traditional aspects of the culture do not change as dramatically just because Latinas are in advanced education or have married out of the culture. These Latinas felt strong connections (both positive and undecided) to traditional culture. For example, gender roles for females in the family were understood but not always agreed upon, the understanding of the supernatural in their lives and their strong feelings about their families of origin contributed to these connections.

Latinas' families are first priority in many instances. Educators and helping professionals should understand the importance of including the family whenever possible. Many of these women attributed their success to the sacrifices that their families have made for them. All of these Latinas identified themselves as helping professionals. They desired to give back to the Latino community as much as possible. The author suggests that the empowerment definition stated earlier in this text is very true. Women of color become empowered as individuals, and become involved in the group process of empowerment which in turn, empowers other individual women. The approach is circular and creates opportunities for women of color to see other women of color and their success. Educators and helping professionals should understand and support the importance of helping others, that these Latinas demonstrated and also their commitment to the Latino community by developing relevant information designed to attract Latinas to the helping professions and community work.

Catholic education for their daughters was a prominent choice of some of these Latino parents. The presenting question should be to Catholic educators, how are Latinas' educational and social needs being met currently met in Catholic education curricula? These Latinas believed in God, Higher Powers, and spiritual guides to assist them in their daily lives. It seemed to be far more acceptable to rely on intuition, fate, supernatural forces and the unexplainable to guide some decisions that these Latinas made. Attempting to provide as much support to Latinas, the researcher suggests that educators and helping professionals study cultural sensitive approaches to problem solving, and their unique nature, as they relate to Mexican American women. Why are these historias of Latina women important? The historias are important because they provide thick, rich and authentic detail of these Latinas' lives. The stories expose their dreams (literally) and their painful recollections that have molded them into the women they are today. Educators, helping professionals, social scientists, and others should give serious attention to Latinas' lives as conveyed in this context of qualitative research called hermeneutic phenomenology. Van Manen (1990) describes this approach as a philosophy of the personal, the individual, which is understood through pursuit of the logos of other, the whole, the communal, or the social (p. 7). This type of research is not intended to prove or generalize groups of Latinas in order to explain their behavior or provide taxonomic indices. What this research can do is provide the reader with an intimate look at these Latinas' lives. The reader is able to generate for him or herself how these lives interrelate. These life histories capture the Mexican-American woman experience. Latina women are on the forefront of every major social system today. How professional educators and social scientists approach Latina women and learn more about the culture, will indicate to Latina women the sincerity (sinceridad), the humility (humilidad) and the respect (respeto) that we show them by "diciendo sus cuentos" (telling their stories), in the manner in which they've told us.

## REFERENCES

Blea, I. (1992). La Chicana and the Intersection of Race, Class, and Gender. New York: Praeger Press.

Blea, I. (1997). U.S. Chicanas and Latinas Within A Global Context: Women of Color at the Fourth World Women's Conference. Westport, CT: Praeger.

Buriel, R. (1982). Relationship of Traditional Mexican American Culture to Adjustment and Delinquency Among Three Generations of Mexican American Male Adolescents. Hispanic Journal of Behavioral Sciences, 1, 41–55.

Cummins, J. (1986). Empowering Minority Students: A framework for intervention. Harvard Educational Review, 56, 18–36.

del Portillo, C.T. (1988). Poverty, Self-Concept and Health: Experience of Latinas. San Francisco: The Haworth Press, Inc.

DiNitto, D.M., & McNeece, C.A. (1990). Social Work Issues and Opportunities in a Challenging Profession. Englewood Cliffs, NJ: Prentice-Hall Inc.

Gandara, P. (1982). Passing through the eye of the needle: High Achieving Chicanas. Hispanic Journal of Behavioral Sciences, 4(2), 167–179.

Garcia, A.M. (1990). Studying Chicanas: Bringing Women into the Frame of Chicano Studies. In T. Cordova, Cantu, N., Cardenas, G., Garcia, J., & Sierra, C. (Eds.), Chicana Voices: Intersections of Class, Race and Gender (pp. 19–29). Albuquerque: University of New Mexico Press.

Gutierrez, Lorraine M. (1990). Working with Women of Color: An Empowerment Perspective. Social Work. March. 149–153.

Mandelbaum, D.H. (1973). The Study of Life History: Gandhi. Current Anthropology, 14, 177–206.

Marshall, C. & Rossman, G. (1989). Designing Qualitative Research. Newbury Park, CA: Sage.

Merriam, S.B. (1988). The Case Study Research in Education. San Francisco: Jossey-Bass.

Ramirez, M. & Price-Williams, D.R. (1974). Cognitive Styles of Children of Three Ethnic Groups in the United States. Journal of Cross-Cultural Psychology, 5(2), 212–219.

Rueschenberg, E., & Buriel, R. (1989). Mexican American Family Functioning and Acculturation: A Family Systems Perspective. Hispanic Journal of Behavioral Sciences, 11(3), 232–244.

Senour, M.N. (1977). Psychology of the Chicana. In J.L. Martinez (Ed.), Chicano Psychology. New York: Academic Press.

Van Manen, M. (1990). Researching Lived Experience: Human Service for an Action Sensitive Pedagogy. New York: The State University of New York Press.

Vasquez, M. (1982). Confronting Barriers to the Participation of Mexican- American Women in Higher Education. Hispanic Journal of Behavioral Sciences, 4(2), 147–165.

Watson, L.C. & Watson-Franke, M.B. (1985). Interpreting Life Histories. New Brunswick, NJ: Rutgers University Press.

APPENDIX

# Text Base Alpha Codes

T HE TABLE PRESENTED REPRESENTS THE CODES THAT THE AUTHOR IDENTIFIED WHILE coding the Latinas' life histories. Shown in the table are the frequency of occurrence and lines of text represented in each code. For example, the reader may wish to see how much content attention that Ramona gave to the code intuition. The reader would then find Ramona's codes and find that intuition was discussed in length. If the reader chose they could find demographic variables and code relationships to see if there were any strong patterns that could emerge. For example, birth order and the code success may suggest that in the family, birth order is important when one discusses success. The purpose of this table is to provide the reader with descriptive codes suggested by the author, utilize the demographic variables, and generate questions for research for both qualitative and quantitative approaches in the future.

| | | Informant | | | | | | | |
|---|---|---|---|---|---|---|---|---|---|
| | Carmen | Chonita | Eufemia | Ramona | Mary | Gloria | Aurora | Leorita | Carolina |
| **Demographic** | | | | | | | | | |
| Age | 31 | 36 | 37 | 38 | 29 | 28 | 23 | 37 | 33 |
| Marital | d | d | m | m | s | m | s | m | m |
| Birth Order | 2 | 3 | 3 | 3 | 5 | 6 | 3 | 1 | 1 |
| Cultural | me | me | me | la | me | me | hi | me | ch |
| Education | 16 | 17 | 14 | 16 | 16 | 17 | 17 | 12 | 18 |
| Religion | none | ca | ca | none | ca | ca | none | ca | ca |
| Children | 1 | 2 | 1 | 0 | 0 | 1 | 0 | 4 | 0 |
| Generation | 3 | 3 | 3 | 2 | 3 | 1 | 2 | 2 | 3 |
| Income | 15 | 20 | 15 | 15 | 12 | 15 | 12 | 20 | 20 |
| **TBA Codes** | | | | | **Frequency/Lines of Text** | | | | |
| age | 3/4 | 1/1 | 0/0 | 0/0 | 0/0 | 0/0 | 1/1 | 1/3 | 0/0 |
| artistic | 0/0 | 0/0 | 0/0 | 2/12 | 1/5 | 0/0 | 2/156 | 0/0 | 2/102 |
| attitude | 1/72 | 4/40 | 2/32 | 2/27 | 1/6 | 0/0 | 5/48 | 2/183 | 4/84 |
| bicultural | 0/0 | 2/253 | 0/0 | 0/0 | 1/17 | 0/0 | 0/0 | 2/270 | 0/0 |
| career | 0/0 | 0/0 | 1/26 | 0/0 | 1/7 | 1/3 | 1/18 | 0/0 | 1/17 |
| catholic | 0/0 | 0/0 | 0/0 | 2/7 | 1/5 | 2/26 | 0/0 | 1/124 | 1/5 |
| children | 0/0 | 2/97 | 0/0 | 0/0 | 0/0 | 0/0 | 0/0 | 1/2 | 0/0 |
| Communicate | 0/0 | 1/29 | 0/0 | 0/0 | 0/0 | 0/0 | 0/0 | 0/0 | 0/0 |
| community | 0/0 | 1/33 | 0/0 | 0/0 | 0/0 | 0/0 | 0/0 | 3/106 | 2/79 |
| complexion | 0/0 | 0/0 | 0/0 | 0/0 | 2/36 | 0/0 | 0/0 | 0/0 | 0/0 |
| culture | 0/0 | 5/202 | 0/0 | 4/69 | 2/45 | 3/82 | 0/0 | 2/19 | 12/28 7 |
| death | 0/0 | 2/72 | 0/0 | 0/0 | 0/0 | 0/0 | 0/0 | 0/0 | 0/0 |
| Discrimination | 0/0 | 0/0 | 0/0 | 0/0 | 0/0 | 1/13 | 1/11 | 2/163 | 3/114 |
| driving | 0/0 | 1/2 | 0/0 | 0/0 | 0/0 | 0/0 | 0/0 | 0/0 | 0/0 |
| education | 1/12 | 2/181 | 4/198 | 0/0 | 1/19 | 1/14 | 1/7 | 2/42 | 3/135 |
| family | 2/75 | 3/230 | 3/121 | 1/45 | 2/23 | 5/130 | 1/58 | 2/88 | 2/69 |
| gender role | 0/0 | 1/76 | 0/0 | 0/0 | 0/0 | 0/0 | 0/0 | 0/0 | 7/124 |
| helping | 1/9 | 0/0 | 1/134 | 1/15 | 0/0 | 0/0 | 2/41 | 1/2 | 1/10 |
| holistic | 0/0 | 0/0 | 0/0 | 1/4 | 0/0 | 0/0 | 1/14 | 0/0 | 0/0 |
| honesty | 1/9 | 0/0 | 0/0 | 0/0 | 0/0 | 0/0 | 0/0 | 0/0 | 0/0 |
| humility | 0/0 | 1/7 | 0/0 | 0/0 | 1/20 | 0/0 | 0/0 | 1/39 | 0/0 |
| intuition | 0/0 | 0/0 | 0/0 | 6/149 | 0/0 | 3/30 | 0/0 | 0/0 | 0/0 |
| intuitive | 0/0 | 1/9 | 0/0 | 0/0 | 0/0 | 0/0 | 1/47 | 1/44 | 1/18 |
| language | 0/0 | 3/206 | 1/13 | 0/0 | 2/58 | 0/0 | 0/0 | 0/0 | 0/0 |
| marriage | 0/0 | 2/78 | 1/34 | 2/14 | 0/0 | 0/0 | 0/0 | 0/0 | 0/0 |

| | Informant | | | | | | | | |
|---|---|---|---|---|---|---|---|---|---|
| | Carmen | Chonita | Eufemia | Ramona | Mary | Gloria | Aurora | Leorita | Carolina |
| matriarchy | 0/0 | 0/0 | 0/0 | 0/0 | 0/0 | 0/0 | 0/0 | 1/1 | 0/0 |
| mexico | 0/0 | 0/0 | 7/92 | 0/0 | 0/0 | 0/0 | 0/0 | 0/0 | 0/0 |
| migrant | 0/0 | 0/0 | 7/92 | 0/0 | 0/0 | 0/0 | 0/0 | 0/0 | 0/0 |
| patriarchy | 0/0 | 0/0 | 1/11 | 2/9 | 0/0 | 1/9 | 0/0 | 0/0 | 2/14 |
| rolemodel | 0/0 | 0/0 | 2/89 | 1/21 | 3/64 | 1/13 | 0/0 | 2/274 | 4/136 |
| self id | 0/0 | 0/0 | 3/107 | 1/9 | 0/0 | 0/0 | 3/30 | 0/0 | 3/141 |
| spirituality | 1/8 | 0/0 | 2/131 | 1/44 | 1/56 | 1/12 | 1/16 | 3/75 | 0/0 |
| success | 2/36 | 1/69 | 1/29 | 1/103 | 1/33 | 2/54 | 2/98 | 0/0 | 2/49 |
| traditional | 0/0 | 0/0 | 1/144 | 0/0 | 2/26 | 0/0 | 0/0 | 1/51 | 0/0 |
| turning point | 5/342 | 2/109 | 2/120 | 0/0 | 3/44 | 1/49 | 5/124 | 0/0 | 4/84 |

# References

Agar, M.H. (1980). The Professional Stranger: An Informal Introduction to Ethnography. New York: Academic Press.

Andrade, S. (1982). Social Science Stereotypes of the Mexican American Woman: Policy Implications for Research. Hispanic Journal of Behavioral Sciences, 4(2), 223–244.

Arias, M.B. (1986). The Context of Education for Hispanic Students: An Overview. American Journal of Education, 95,26–57.

Augenbraum, H. & Stavans, I. (1993). Growing Up Latino. Boston: Houghton Mifflin Company.

Becerra, R.M., Karno, M. & Escobar, J.I. (1982). The Hispanic Patient: Mental Health Perspectives. New York: Grune and Stratton, Inc.

Berry, J.W. (1980). Acculturation as Varieties of Adaptation. In A.M. Padilla (Ed.), Acculturation: Theory, Models, and Some New Findings. Boulder, CO: Westview Press.

Berry, J.W., & Annis, R.C. (1974). Acculturative Stress: The Role of Ecology, Culture, and Differentiation. Journal of Cross-Cultural Psychology, 5, 382–406.

Blea, Irene I. (1997). U.S. Chicanas and Latinas Within A Global Context: Women of Color at the Fourth World Women's Conference. Westport, CT: Praeger.

Blea, Irene I. (1992). La Chicana and the Intersection of Race, Class, and Gender. New York: Praeger Press.

Bogden, R.C., & Biklen, S.K. (1992). Qualitative Research for Education. Needham Heights, MA: Allyn and Bacon.

Bonilla-Santiago, Gloria. (1991). Hispanic Women Breaking New Ground Through Leadership. Latino Studies Journal, 2, 19–37.

Buriel, R. (1982). Relationship of Traditional Mexican American Culture to Adjustment and Delinquency Among Three Generations of Mexican

American Male Adolescents. Hispanic Journal of Behavioral Sciences, 1, 41–55.

Caetano, R. (1986). Patterns and Problems of Drinking Among U.S. Hispanics. In U.S. Department of Health and Human Services, Report of the Secretary's Task Force on Black and Minority Health. Volume VII, Chemical Dependency and Diabetes (pp. 143–186) (DHHS Publication No. 85–487). Washington, DC: U.S. Government Printing Office.

Canino, G. (1982). The Hispanic Woman: Sociocultural influences on diagnoses and treatment. In R. M. Becerra, M. Karno & J.I. Escobar (Eds)., Mental Health and Hispanic Americans (pp. 117–137). New York: Grune and Stratton, Inc.

Church, G. (1985, July 8). Hispanics: A Melding of Cultures. Time, p. 36.

Comas-Diaz, L., & Greene, B. (1994). Women of Color with Professional Status. In L. Comas-Diaz & B. Greene (Eds.), Women of Color: Integrating ethnic and gender identities in psychotherapy (pp. 347–388). New York: Guilford Press.

Cotera, M. Profile on the Mexican American Woman. Austin, TX: National Educational Laboratory, 1976.

Cuellar, I., Harris, L.C., & Jasso, R. (1980). An Acculturation Rating Scale for Mexican-American Normal and Clinical Populations. Hispanic Journal of Behavioral Sciences, 2, 199–217.

Cummins, J. (1986). Empowering Minority Students: A framework for intervention. Harvard Educational Review, 56, 18–36.

Curtis, P.A. (1990). The Consequences of Acculturation to Service Delivery and Research with Hispanic Families. Child and Adolescent Social Work Journal, 7(2), 147–159.

Das Surya Lama. (1997). Eight Steps to Enlightenment: Awakening the Buddha Within Tibetan Wisdom for the Western World. New York: Broadway Books.

del Portillo, C.T. (1988). Poverty, Self-Concept and Health: Experience of Latinas. San Francisco: The Haworth Press, Inc.

Diaz-Guerrero, R. (1955). Neurosis and the Mexican Family Structure. American Journal of Psychiatry, 112, 411–417.

DiNitto, D.M. & McNeece, C.A. (1990). Social Work Issues and Opportunities in a Challenging Profession. Englewood Cliffs, N.J: Prentice-Hall Inc.

Gandara, P. (1982). Passing through the eye of the needle: High Achieving Chicanas. Hispanic Journal of Behavioral Sciences, 4(2), 167–179.

Garcia, J.G. & Zea, M.C. (1997). Psychological Interventions and Research with Latino Populations. Boston: Allyn and Bacon.

Garcia, A.M. (1990). Studying Chicanas: Bringing Women into the Frame of Chicano Studies. In T. Cordova, Cantu, N., Cardenas, G., Garcia, J., & Sierra, C (Eds.), Chicana Voices: Intersections of Class, Race and Gender (pp. 19–29). Albuquerque: University of New Mexico Press.

Garza, R.T., & Lipton, J.P. (1982). Theoretical Perspectives on Chicano Personality Development. Hispanic Journal of Behavioral Sciences, 4(4), 407–432.

Goetz, J.P., & Le Compte, M.D. (1984). Ethnography and Qualitative Design in Educational Research. New York: Academic Press.

Gracia, Jorge J.E. & Greiff, P. (2000). Hispanics/Latinos in the United States. New York: Routledge.

Griffith, J. (1983). Relationship Between Acculturation and Psychological Impairment in Adult Mexican Americans. Hispanic Journal of Behavioral Sciences, 5, 431–459.

Gutierrez, Lorraine M. (1990). Working with Women of Color: An Empowerment Perspective. Social Work. March. 149–153.

Gusdorf, Georges. Conditions and Limits of Autobiography. In James Olney (Ed.), Autobiography: Essays Theoretical and Cultural (pp. 28–48). Princeton: Princeton University Press.

Helms, J.E. (1990). Black and White Racial Identity: Theory, Research, and Practice. New York: Greenwood Press.

Hoare, C. (1991). Psychosocial Identity Development and Cultural Others. Journal of Counseling & Development. September/October 1991, 70, 45–53.

Humm-Delgado, D. & Delgado, M. Hispanic Adolescents and Substance Abuse: Issues for the 1980s. In Adolescent Substance Abuse (pp. 71–85). Haworth Press, 1983.

Jacob, E. (1987). Traditions of Qualitative Research: A Review. Review of Educational Research, 51, 1–50.

Kiev, A. (1972). Transcultural Psychiatry. New York: The Free Press.

Kluckhohn, F.R. & Strodtbeck, F.L. (1961). Variations in Value Orientations. Evanston, IL: Row, Patterson, & Co.

Kranau, E.J., Green, V. & Valencia-Weber, G. (1982). Acculturation and the Hispanic Woman: Attitudes Toward Women, Sex-Role Attribution, Sex-Role Behavior, and Demographics. Hispanic Journal of Behavioral Sciences, 4(1), 21–40.

Lama, Surya Das. (1997). Awakening the Buddha Within. New York: Broadway Books.

Lacayo, R. 1988. "A Surging New Spirit". Time, Vol. 132 (July 11): 46–49.

Locke, Don C. (1992). Increasing Multicultural Understanding. Newbury Park, CA: Sage.

Mandelbaum, D.H. (1973). The Study of Life History: Gandhi. Current Anthropology, 14, 177–206.

Marshall, C. & Rossman, G. (1989). Designing Qualitative Research. Newbury Park, CA: Sage.

Martinez, M.A. (1981). Conversational Asymmetry Between Mexican Mothers and Children. Hispanic Journal of Behavioral Sciences, 3, 329–346.

Martinez, M.A. (1986). Family Socialization Among Mexican-Americans. Human Development, 29, 264–279.

Martinez, Marcos, A. (1988). Toward A Model of Socialization for Hispanic Identity: The Case of Mexican-Americans. In Pastora San Juan Cafferty & W.L. McCready (Eds), Hispanics in the United States. New Jersey: Transaction Books.

Maslow, A. (1968). Synergy in the Society and in the Individual. Journal of Individual Psychology, 20, 153–164.

Mendoza, R.H., & Martinez, J.L. (1981). The Measurement of Acculturation. In A. Baron Jr. (Ed.), Exploration in Chicano Psychology. New York: Holt Press.

Merriam, S.B. (1988). The Case Study Research in Education. San Francisco: Jossey-Bass.

Miles, M.S., & Huberman, A.M. (1984). Qualitative Data Analysis: A Sourcebook of New Methods. Beverly Hills, CA: Sage.

Nebraska Department of Health and Human Services Preventive and Community Health. (2000). Health Status of Racial and Ethnic Minorities in Nebraska: Preliminary Findings.

Padilla, A.M., & Ruiz, R.A. Latino Mental Health: A Review of the Literature. National Institute of Mental Health, Washington, DC: U.S. Government Printing Office, 1973.

Ramirez, M. III. (1998). Multicultural/Multiracial Psychology: Mestizo Perspectives in Personality and Mental Health. Northvale, NJ: Jason Aronson Inc.

Ramirez, M., & Castaneda, A. (1974). Cultural Democracy, Bicognitive Development, and Education. New York: Academic Press.

Ramirez, M. & Price-Williams, D.R. (1974). Cognitive Styles of Children of Three Ethnic Groups in the United States. Journal of Cross-Cultural Psychology, 5(2), 212–219.

Ramirez, M. (1984). Assessing and Understanding Biculturalism-Multiculturalism in Mexican-American Adults. In J.L. Martinez & R.H. Mendoza (Eds.), Chicano Psychology, 2nd Ed. (pp. 77–94) Orlando, FL: Academic Press.

Ramirez, R. (1990). The Application of Adult Education to Community Development. Community Development Journal, 23(2), 131–138.

Rappaport, J. (1985). The Power of Empowerment Language. Social Policy, 17(2), 15–21.

Rueschenberg, E., & Buriel, R. (1989). Mexican American Family Functioning and Acculturation: A Family Systems Perspective. Hispanic Journal of Behavioral Sciences, 11(3), 232–244.

Sabogal, F.,G. Marin, R. Otero-Sabogal, B.V. Marin, & E.J. Perez-Stable. (1987). Hispanic Familism and Acculturation: What changes and what doesn't? Hispanic Journal of Behavioral Sciences, 9, 397–412.

Satterfield, D.M. Acculturation and marriage role patterns: A comparative study of Mexican American Women. Unpublished doctoral dissertation, University of Arizona, 1966.

Schatzman, L., & Strauss, A. (1973). Field Research: Strategies for a Natural Sociology. Englewood Cliffs, NJ: Prentice-Hall.

Schweder, R.A. (1991). Thinking Through Cultures. Cambridge: Harvard University Press.

Senour, M.N. (1977). Psychology of the Chicana. In J.L. Martinez (Ed.), Chicano Psychology. New York: Academic Press.

Spradley, James P. 1980. Participant Observation. Macalester College: Holt, Rinehart, and Winston, Inc.

Stanley, S.K. (1998). Other Sisterhoods. Chicago: University of Illinois Press.

Sundberg, N.D. (1981). Cross-Cultural Counseling and Psychotherapy: A Research Overview. In A.J. Marsella and P.B. Pederson (Eds.), Cross-Cultural Counseling and Psychotherapy. New York: Pergamon Press.

Tesch, R. 1989. Textbase Alpha User's Manual. Qualitative Research Management. Desert Hot Springs, CA.

Tharp, R.G., Meadow, A., Lennhoff, S.G., & Satterfield, D.M. (1968). Changes in marriage roles accompanying the acculturation of the Mexican American wife. Journal of Marriage and the Family, 30, 404–412.

Torres-Matrullo, C.M. (1980). Acculturation, sex-role values and mental health among mainland Puerto Ricans. In A.M. Padilla (Ed.), Acculturation: Theory, Models, and Some New Findings. Boulder, CO: Westview Press.

University of California at Los Angeles: Summer 1990, Qualitative Research Seminar for Latino Doctoral Students.

U.S. Bureau of the Census, U.S. Population Estimates Program, Population Division. (2000, October). Resident Population Estimates of the United States by Sex, Race, and Hispanic Origin: April 1, 1990 to July 1, 1999, with Short-Term Projection to September 1, 2000. Washington, DC: U.S. Government Printing Office.

Van Manen, M. (1990). Researching Lived Experience: Human Service for an Action Sensitive Pedagogy. New York: The State University of New York Press.

Vasquez, M. (1982). Confronting Barriers to the Participation of Mexican-American Women in Higher Education. Hispanic Journal of Behavioral Sciences, 4(2), 147–165.

Watson, L.C. & Watson-Franke, M.B. (1985). Interpreting Life Histories. New Brunswick, NJ: Rutgers University Press.

Whorf, B.L. (1956). Science and Linguistics. In J.B. Carroll (Ed.), Language, Thought, and Reality (pp. 212–213). Cambridge: Technology Press of Massachusetts Institute of Technology.

Ybarra, L. (1983). Empirical and Theoretical Developments in the Study of Chicano Families. In A. Valdez, A. Camarillo, and T. Almaguer (Eds.),

The State of Chicano Research on Family, Labor, and Migration. Stanford: Stanford Center for Chicano Research.

Zuniga, M.E. (1988). Assessment Issues with Chicanas: Practice Implications. Psychotherapy, 25(2), 288–293.

# Index